Research Skills Projects

Phil Schlemmer

Illustrated by Patricia A. Sussman

LEARNING ON YOUR OWN!

Individual, Group, and Classroom
Research Projects for
Gifted and Motivated Students

The Center for Applied Research in Education, Inc.
West Nyack, New York

10 9 8 7 6 5

Library of Congress Cataloging-in-Publication Data

Schlemmer, Phillip L.
  Research skills projects.

  (Learning on your own: unit 1)
   1. Independent study. 2. Project method in teaching.
3. Research—Methodology—Study and teaching (Elementary)
4. School children—Library orientation. 5. Curriculum
enrichment. 6. Gifted children—Education (Elementary)—
Curricula—Handbooks, manuals, etc. I. Title
II. Series: Schlemmer, Phillip L. Learning on your own!
LC3993.22.S34   1987   372.13'943   86-13713

ISBN 0-87628-508-6

PRINTED IN THE UNITED STATES OF AMERICA

Dedication

This book is dedicated to my wife, Dori. Without her unending support, tireless editorial efforts, thoughtful criticisms, and patience, I could not have finished my work. Thank you, Dori.

Acknowledgments

My collaborator and co-teacher for eight years, Dennis Kretschman, deserves special mention at this juncture. Together we developed the activities, projects, and courses that became a "learning to learn" curriculum. Dennis designed and taught several of the projects described in these pages, and he added constantly to the spirit and excitement of an independent learning philosophy that gradually evolved into this set of five books. I deeply appreciate the contribution Dennis has made to my work.

I would also like to thank the following people for their advice, support, and advocacy: J. Q. Adams; Dr. Robert Barr; Robert Cole, Jr.; Mary Dalheim; Dr. John Feldhusen; David Humphrey; Bruce Ottenweller; Dr. William Parrett; Ed Saunders; Charles Whaley; and a special thanks to all the kids who have attended John Ball Zoo School since I started working on this project: 1973–1985.

About the Author

PHIL SCHLEMMER, M.Ed., has been creating and teaching independent learning projects since 1973, when he began his master's program in alternative education at Indiana University. Assigned to Grand Rapids, Michigan, for his internship, he helped develop a full-time school for 52 motivated sixth graders. The school was located at the city zoo and immediately became known as the "Zoo School." This program became an experimental site where he remained through the 1984–85 school year, with one year out as director of a high school independent study program.

Presently working as a private consultant, Mr. Schlemmer has been presenting in-services and workshops to teachers, parents, administrators, and students for more than 13 years and has published articles in *Phi Delta Kappan* and *Instructor*.

Foreword

This series of books will become invaluable aids in programs for motivated, gifted, and talented children. They provide clear guidelines and procedures for involving these children in significant learning experiences in research and high level thinking skills while not neglecting challenging learning within the respective basic disciplines of science, mathematics, social studies, and writing. The approach is one that engages the interests of children at a deep level. I have seen Phil Schlemmer at work teaching with the materials and methods presented in these books and have been highly impressed with the quality of learning which was taking place. While I recognized Phil is an excellent teacher, it nevertheless seemed clear that the method and the materials were making a strong and significant contribution to the children's learning.

Children will learn how to carry out research and will become independent lifelong learners through the skills acquired from the program of studies presented in these books. Success in independent study and research and effective use of libraries and other information resources are not simply products of trial-and-error activity in school. They are products of teacher guidance and stimulation along with instructional materials and methods and an overall system which provides the requisite skills and attitudes.

All of the material presented in this series of books has undergone extensive tryout. The author has also spent thousands of hours developing, writing, revising, and editing, but above all he has spent his time conceptualizing and designing a dynamic system for educating motivated, gifted, and talented youth. The net result is a program of studies which should make an invaluable contribution to the education of these youth. And, above all that, I am sure that if it is taught well, the kids will love it.

John F. Feldhusen, Ph.D., Director
Gifted Education Resource Institute
Purdue University
West Lafayette, Indiana 47907

About Learning on Your Own!

In the summer of 1973, I was offered the opportunity of a lifetime. The school board in Grand Rapids, Michigan authorized a full-time experimental program for 52 motivated sixth-grade children, and I was asked to help start it. The school was described as an environmental studies program, and its home was established in two doublewide house trailers that were connected and converted into classrooms. This building was placed in the parking lot of Grand Rapids' municipal zoo (John Ball Zoological Gardens). Naturally, the school came to be known as "The Zoo School."

The mandate for the Zoo School staff was clear—to build a challenging, stimulating, and interesting curriculum that was in no way limited by the school system's stated sixth-grade objectives. Operating with virtually no textbooks or "regular" instructional materials, we had the freedom to develop our own projects and courses, schedule our own activities, and design our own curriculum.

Over a period of ten years, hundreds of activities were created to use with motivated learners. This was a golden opportunity because few teachers are given a chance to experiment with curriculum in an isolated setting with the blessing of the school board. When a project worked, I wrote about it, recorded the procedures that were successful, filed the handouts, and organized the materials so that someone else could teach it. The accumulation of projects for motivated children led to a book proposal which, in turn, led to this five-book series. *Learning on Your Own!* is based entirely on actual classroom experience. Every project and activity has been used successfully with children in the areas of

- Research Skills
- Writing
- Science
- Mathematics
- Social Studies

As the books evolved and materialized over the years, it seemed that they would be useful to classroom teachers, especially in the upper and elementary and junior high grades. This became increasingly clear as teachers from a wide variety of settings were presented with ideas from the books. Teachers saw different uses for the projects, based upon the abilities of their students and their own curricular needs.

Learning on Your Own! will be useful to you for any of the following reasons:

- If a curricular goal is to teach children to be independent learners, then skill development is necessary. The projects in each book are arranged according to the level of independence that is required—the early projects can be used to *teach* skills; the later ones require their *use*.

- These projects prepare the way for students confidently to make use of higher-level thinking skills.

- A broad range of students can benefit from projects that are skill-oriented. They need not be gifted/talented.

- On the other hand, teachers of the gifted/talented will see that the emphasis on independence and higher-level thinking makes the projects fit smoothly into their curricular goals.

- The projects are designed for use by one teacher with a class of up to 30 students. They are intentionally built to accommodate the "regular" classroom teacher. Projects that require 1-to-1 or even 1-to-15 teacher-student ratios are of little use to most teachers.

- The books do not represent a curriculum that must be followed. Gifted/talented programs may have curricula based upon the five-book series, and individual situations may allow for the development of a "learning to learn" curriculum. Generally speaking, however, each project is self-contained and need not be a part of a year-long progression of courses and projects.

- Each project offers a format that can be used even if the *content* is changed. You may, with some modification, apply many projects toward subject material that is already being taught. This provides a means of delivering the same message in a different way.

- Most teachers have students in their classes capable of pursuing projects that are beyond the scope of the class as a whole. These books can be used to provide special projects for such students so that they may learn on their own.

- One of the most pervasive concepts in *Learning on Your Own!* is termed "kids teaching kids." Because of the emphasis placed on students teaching one another, oral presentations are required for many projects. This reinforces the important idea that not only can students *learn,* they can also *teach.* Emphasis on oral presentation can be reduced if time constraints demand it.

- The premise of this series is that children, particularly those who are motivated to learn, need a base from which to expand their educational horizons. Specifically, this base consists of five important components of independent learning:

—skills
—confidence
—a mandate to pursue independence

—projects that show students *how* to learn on their own

—an opportunity to practice independent learning

Learning on Your Own! places primary emphasis on the motivated learner, the definition of which is left intentionally ambiguous. It is meant to include most normal children who have natural curiosities and who understand the need for a good education. Motivated children are important people who deserve recognition for their ability and desire to achieve. The trend toward understanding the special needs and incredible potential of children who enjoy the adventure and challenge of learning is encouraging. Teachers, parents, business people, community leaders, and concerned citizens are beginning to seriously ask, "What can we do for these young people who want to learn?"

Creating a special program or developing a new curriculum is not necessarily the answer. Many of the needs of these children can be met in the regular classroom by teaching basic independent learning skills. No teacher can possibly master and teach all of the areas that his or her students may be interested in studying, but every teacher has opportunities to place emphasis on basic learning skills. A surprising number of children become more motivated as they gain skills that allow them to learn independently. "Learning on your own" is an important concept because it, in itself, provides motivation. You can contribute to your students' motivation by emphasizing self-confidence and skill development. One simple project during a semester can give students insight into the usefulness of independent learning. One lesson that emphasizes a skill can bring students a step closer to choosing topics, finding information, planning projects, and making final presentations without assistance. By teaching motivated students *how to learn on their own,* you give them the ability to challenge themselves, to transcend the six-hour school day.

Beyond meeting the immediate needs of individual students, teaching children how to learn on their own will have an impact on their adult lives and may affect society itself. It is easy to discuss the day-to-day importance of independent learning in one breath, and in the next be talking of the needs of adults 30 years from now. This five-book series is based upon the assumption that educating children to be independent learners makes sense in a complicated, rapidly changing, unpredictable world. Preparing today's children for tomorrow's challenges is of paramount importance to educators and parents, but a monumental task lies in deciding what can be taught that will have lasting value in years to come. What will people need to know in the year 2001 and beyond? Can we accurately prescribe a set of facts and information that will be *necessary* to an average citizen 10, 20, or 30 years from now? Can we feel confident that what we teach will be useful, or even relevant, by the time our students become adults? Teaching children to be independent learners is a compelling response to these difficult, thought-provoking questions.

How to Use
Learning on Your Own!

Learning on Your Own! can be used in many ways. The projects and the overall design of the books lend themselves to a variety of applications, such as basic skill activities, full-class units or courses, small-group projects, independent study, and even curriculum development. Regardless of how the series is to be implemented, it is important to understand its organization and recognize what it provides. Like a good cookbook, this series supplies more than a list of ingredients. It offers suggestions, advice, and hints; provides organization and structure; and gives time lines, handouts, and materials lists. In other words, it supplies everything necessary for you to conduct the projects.

These books were produced with you in mind. Every project is divided into three general sections to provide uniformity throughout the series and to give each component a standard placement in the material. The first section, Teacher Preview, gives a brief overview of the scope and focus of the project. The second section, Lesson Plans and Notes, outlines a detailed, hour-by-hour description. After reading this, every nuance of the project should be understood. The third section, Instructional Materials, supplies the "nuts-and-bolts" of the project—reproducible assignment sheets, instructional handouts, tests, answer sheets, and evaluations.

Here is a concise explanation of each of the three sections. Read this material before going further to better understand how the projects can be used.

Teacher Preview

The Teacher Preview is a quick explanation of what a project accomplishes or teaches. It is divided into seven areas, each of which provides specific information about the project:

Length of Project: The length of each project is given in classroom hours. It does not take into account homework or teacher-preparation time.

Level of Independence: Each project is identified as "basic," "intermediate," or "advanced" in terms of how much independence is required of students. The level of independence is based primarily on how many decisions a student must make and how much responsibility is required. It is suggested that students who have not acquired independent learning skills, regardless of their grade level, be carefully introduced to advanced projects.

For teachers who are interested, there is a correlation between the skill development mentioned here and the progression to higher-level thinking skills typified by Benjamin Bloom's "Taxonomy of Educational Objectives":

Level of Independence	Bloom's Taxonomy
Basic	Knowledge Comprehension
Intermediate	Application Analysis
Advanced	Synthesis Evaluation

Goals: These are straightforward statements of what a project is designed to accomplish. Goals that recur throughout the series deal with skill development, independent learning, and "kids teaching kids."

During This Project Students Will: This is a list of concise project objectives. Occasionally, some of these statements become activities rather than objectives, but they are included because they help specify what students will do during the course of a project.

Skills: Each project emphasizes a specific set of skills, which are listed in this section. Further information about the skills is provided in the "Skills Chart." You may change the skill emphasis of a project according to curricular demands or the needs of the students.

Handouts Provided: The handouts provided with a project are listed by name. This includes assignment sheets, informational handouts, tests, and evaluation forms.

Project Calendar: This is a chart that graphically shows each hour of instruction. Since it does not necessarily represent consecutive days, lines are provided for you to pencil in dates. The calendar offers a synopsis of each hour's activity and also brief notes to clue you about things that must be done:

PREPARATION REQUIRED   STUDENTS TURN IN WORK

NEED SPECIAL MATERIALS   RETURN STUDENT WORK

HANDOUT PROVIDED   ANSWER SHEET PROVIDED

Lesson Plans and Notes

The lesson plan is a detailed hour-by-hour description of a project, explaining its organization and presentation methods. Projects can be shortened by reducing the time spent on such things as topic selection, research, and presentation; however, this necessitates de-emphasizing skills that make real independent study possible. Alternately, a project may require additional hours if students are weak in particular skill areas or if certain concepts are not thoroughly understood.

Each hour's lesson plan is accompanied by notes about the project. Some notes are fairly extensive if they are needed to clarify subject matter or describe a process.

Instructional Material

There are five types of reproducible instructional materials included in *Learning on Your Own!* Most projects can be run successfully with just a Student Assignment Sheet; the rest of the materials are to be used as aids at your discretion.

Student Assignment Sheets: Virtually every project has an assignment sheet that explains the project and outlines requirements.

Additional Handouts: Some projects offer other handouts to supply basic information or provide a place to record answers or research data.

Tests and Quizzes: Tests and quizzes are included with projects that present specific content. Since most projects are individualized, the activities themselves are designed to test student comprehension and skill development.

Evaluation Sheets: Many projects provide their own evaluation sheets. In addition, the Teacher's Introduction to the Student Research Guide (see the Appendix) contains evaluations for notecards, posters, and oral presentations. Some projects also supply self-evaluation forms so that students can evaluate their own work.

Forms, Charts, Lists: These aids are provided throughout the series. They are designed for specific situations in individual projects.

OTHER FEATURES OF
LEARNING ON YOUR OWN!

In addition to the projects, each book in the series offers several other useful features:

Grade Level: A grade level notation of upper elementary, junior high, and/or high is shown next to each project in the table of contents. Because this series was developed with gifted/talented/motivated sixth graders, junior high is the logical grade level for most projects; thus, generally speaking, these projects are most appropriate for students in grades 6–8.

Skills Chart: This is a chart listing specific independent learning skills that may be applied to each project. It is fully explained in its introductory material.

Teacher's Introduction to the Student Research Guide: This introduction is found in the Appendix. It offers suggestions for conducting research projects and provides several evaluation forms.

Student Research Guide: Also found in the Appendix, this is a series of checklists that can be used by students working on individualized projects. The Daily Log, for example, is a means of having students keep track of their own progress. In addition to the checklists, there are instructional handouts on basic research skills.

General Notes

Examine the *structure* of the projects in each book, even if the titles do not fit specific needs. Many projects are so skill-oriented that content can be drastically altered without affecting the goals.

Many projects are dependent upon resource materials; the more sources of information, the better. Some way of providing materials for the classroom are to

- Ask parents for donations of books and magazines.
- Advertise for specific materials in the classified section of the newspaper.
- Check out library materials for a mini-library in the classroom.
- Gradually purchase useful materials as they are discovered.
- Take trips to public libraries and make use of school libraries.

Students may not initially recognize the value of using notecards. They will soon learn, however, that the cards allow data to be recorded as individual facts that can be arranged and rearranged at will.

"Listening" is included as an important skill in most projects. In lecture situations, class discussions, and when students are giving presentations, you should require students to listen and respect the right of others to listen.

Provide time for grading and returning materials to students during the course of a project. The Project Calendar is convenient for planning a schedule.

A visual display is often a requirement for projects in this series. Students usually choose to make a poster, but there are other possibilities:

mural	collage	demonstration	dramatization
mobile	model	display or exhibit	book, magazine, or pamphlet
diorama	puppet show	slide show	

When students work on their own, your role changes from information supplier to learning facilitator. It is also important to help students solve their own problems so that momentum and forward progress are maintained.

A FINAL NOTE FROM THE AUTHOR

Learning on Your Own! provides the materials and the structure that are necessary for individualized learning. The only missing elements are the enthusiasm, vitality, and creative energy that are needed to ignite a group of students and set them diligently to work on projects that require concentration and perseverance. I hope that *my* work will make *your* work easier by letting you put your efforts into quality and innovation. The ability to learn independently is perhaps the greatest gift that can be conferred upon students. Give it with the knowledge that it is valuable beyond price, uniquely suited to each individual, and good for a lifetime!

Phil Schlemmer

About This Book

Research is one of those areas that few people take the time to teach. Yet, as students get older, many teachers require the use of research skills for project work. Research skills are to a motivated learner what dribbling and passing skills are to a gifted basketball player—the means to an end. How else is a ballplayer to play? How else is a student to learn? This book emphasizes basic skills, the fundamentals that make it possible to be an independent learner.

The most basic skill-oriented projects (Notecard-Bibliography, Information Search, Letter Writing, Using the Telephone, and Library Projects) are geared toward full class use. They can be modified if they are to be used with only a few students. These are followed by four intermediate research projects (American History, Native Americans, World History, and The World of Science and Inventions). The rest of the projects (Openings, Kids Teaching Kids, That Was the Year, and Independent Project) are advanced and flexible enough to be used with a few individuals, several small groups, or an entire class. Much of the material can be applied to concepts that are already being taught, so this book is valuable to a variety of classroom teachers.

Research is the key to most individualized learning. Given students who have been taught to find and use information independently, a teacher has the luxury to spend time and energy providing a classroom setting where students can, in fact, learn on their own. Remove that given, and the teacher's role becomes one of information provider rather than learning facilitator. This book was not produced to provide independent study projects for children; rather, it was designed to *teach* children how to *become* independent learners. The process of teaching children to use research skills requires a dedicated teacher who understands that a product is always preceded by a process. In this case, the ability to conduct a research project must be preceded by the acquisition of skills, which is what this book is all about.

THE SKILLS CHART

Research Skills Projects is based upon skill development. The projects are arranged according to the amount of independence required, and a list of skills is provided for every project in the book. A comprehensive Skills Chart is included here to help define the skill requirements of each project. Many of them are basic, common-sense skills that are already being taught in your classes.

The Skills Chart is divided into seven general skill areas: research, writing, planning, problem solving, self-discipline, self-evaluation, and presentation. Reading is not included on the chart because it is assumed that reading skills will be used with virtually every project.

The key tells if a skill is prerequisite (#), primary (X), secondary (0), or optional (*) for each project in the book. These designations are based upon the way the projects were originally taught; you may want to shift the skill emphasis of a project to fit the needs of your particular group of students. It is entirely up to you to decide how to present a project and what skills to emphasize. The Skills Chart is only a guide.

Examination of the chart quickly shows which skills are important to a project and which ones may be of secondary value. A project may be changed or rearranged to redirect its skill requirements. The projects in this book are designed to *teach* the use of skills. If a project's Teacher Preview lists twenty skills, but you want to emphasize only three or four of them, that is a perfectly legitimate use of the project.

Evaluating students on their mastery of skills often involves subjective judgments; each student should be evaluated according to his or her *improvement* rather than by comparison with others. Several projects supply evaluation forms to help with this process. In addition, the Teacher's Introduction to the Student Research Guide provides evaluations for notecards, posters, and oral presentations.

A blank Skills Chart is included at the end of the Student Research Guide in the Appendix. This chart can be helpful in several ways:

• Students can chart their own skill progression through a year. Give them a chart and tell them to record the title of a project on the first line. Have them mark the skills *you* have decided to emphasize with the project. This way, students will see *exactly* what skills are being taught and which ones they are expected to know how to use. As projects are continued through the year, the charts will indicate skill development.

• Use the chart to organize the skill emphasis of projects that did not come from this book. Quite often, projects have the potential to teach skills, but they are not organized to do so. An entire course or even a curriculum can be organized according to the skill development on the chart.

• The Skills Chart can be used as a method of reporting to parents. By recording the projects and activities undertaken during a marking period in the left-hand column, a mark for each of the 48 skills can be given. For example, a number system can be used:

1—excellent
2—very good
3—good
4—fair
5—poor

• A simpler method of reporting to parents is to give them a copy of the Skills Chart without marks and use it as the basis for a discussion about skill development.

Finally, most teachers have little or no experience teaching some of the skills listed on the chart. There is plenty of room for experimentation in the field of independent learning, and there are no established "correct" methods of teaching such concepts as problem solving, self-evaluation, and self-discipline. These are things that *can* be taught, but your own teaching style and philosophy will dictate how you choose to do it. The skills listed on this chart should be recognizable as skills that are worth teaching, even if you have not previously emphasized them.

SKILLS CHART: RESEARCH

	# **Prerequisite Skills** Students must have command of these skills.																				

X Primary Skills Students will learn to use these skills; they are necessary to the project.

0 Secondary Skills These skills may play an important role in certain cases.

* Optional Skills These skills may be emphasized but are not required.

	Preparing Bibliographies	Collecting Data	Interviewing	Writing Letters	Library Skills	Listening	Making Notecards	Observing	Summarizing	Grammar	Handwriting	Neatness	Paragraphs	Sentences	Spelling	Group Planning	Organizing	Outlining	Setting Objectives	Selecting Topics
	RESEARCH									**WRITING**						**PLANNING**				
NOTECARD & BIBLIOGRAPHY	X	X			0		X		X	0	X	X	0	0	X		X			*
INFORMATION SEARCH	X	X			X		X		X	*	*	X		*	X		X			
LIBRARY PROJECT	#	X	*	*	X		#		X		X	X				0				0
LETTER WRITING		0	0	X						X	X	X	X	X	X		0			
USING THE TELEPHONE		X	X			X			0		X	0				0				*
AMERICAN HISTORY	#	X	*	*	X		#		X	#	X	X	#	#	X		0	*	*	X
NATIVE AMERICANS	#	X	*	*	X		#		X	#	X	X	#	#	X		0	*	*	X
WORLD HISTORY	#	X	*	*	X		#		X	#	X	X	#	#	X		0	*	*	X
SCIENCE & INVENTIONS	#	X	*	*	X		#		X	#	X	X	#	#	X		0	*	*	X
OPENINGS	#	X	*	*	X	0	#	0	X	#	#	X	#	#	X	X	X	0		X
KIDS TEACHING KIDS	#	X	*	*	X	*	#	*	X	#	#	X	#	#	X		X	X	X	X
THAT WAS THE YEAR	#	X	*	*	#	X	#	X	X	#	#	X	#	#	X	X	X	*	X	X
INDEPENDENT PROJECT	#	#	*	*	#	*	#	*	#	#	#	X	#	#	X		#	#	#	X

xvi

SKILLS CHART: RESEARCH

PROBLEM SOLVING					SELF-DISCIPLINE										SELF-EVALUATION				PRESENTATION								
DIVERGENT-CONVERGENT-EVALUATIVE THINKING	FOLLOWING & CHANGING PLANS	IDENTIFYING PROBLEMS	MEETING DEADLINES	WORKING w/LIMITED RESOURCES	ACCEPTING RESPONSIBILITY	CONCENTRATION	CONTROLLING BEHAVIOR	FOLLOWING PROJECT OUTLINES	INDIVIDUALIZED STUDY HABITS	PERSISTENCE	SHARING SPACE	TAKING CARE OF MATERIALS	TIME MANAGEMENT	WORKING WITH OTHERS	PERSONAL MOTIVATION	SELF-AWARENESS	SENSE OF "QUALITY"	SETTING PERSONAL GOALS	CREATIVE EXPRESSION	CREATING STRATEGIES	DIORAMA & MODEL BUILDING	DRAWING & SKETCHING	POSTER MAKING	PUBLIC SPEAKING	SELF-CONFIDENCE	TEACHING OTHERS	WRITING
									0								0										
							0		X			0					0										
						0			X	0		0	0				*								*		
			0														0										
									X																		
X	0	0	X	0	X	X	X	X	X	X	0	0	X		X	*	X	0	0	X	*	X	X	X	X	X	X
X	0	0	X	0	X	X	X	X	X	X	0	0	X		X	*	X	0	0	X	*	X	X	X	X	X	X
X	0	0	X	0	X	X	X	X	X	X	0	0	X		X	*	X	0	0	X	*	X	X	X	X	X	X
X	0	0	X	0	X	X	X	X	X	X	0	0	X		X	*	X	0	0	X	*	X	X	X	X	X	X
X	X	0	X	0	X	X	X	X	X	X	0	0	X		X	0	X	0	0	X	*	X	X	X	X	X	X
X	X	0	X	0	X	X	X	X	X	X	0	X	X		X	0	X	0	0	X	*	X	X	X	X	X	X
X	X	X	X	X	X	X	X	X	X	X	X	#	X	X	X	X	X	X	X	X	*	X	X	X	X	X	X
X	X	0	X	0	X	X	X	X	X	X	0	#	X		#	0	X	0	0	X	*	X	X	X	X	X	X

Contents

Research Skills Project	Grade Level	Page

NOTECARD-BIBLIOGRAPHY PROJECT

Teacher Preview

Length of Project: 2 hours
Goal: To increase students' research skills
Level of Independence: Basic

During This Project Students Will:

1. Study examples of properly made notecards and bibliographies.
2. Practice writing information on notecards.
3. Discuss, as a class, the importance of accurately recording sources of information used in research.
4. Demonstrate their ability to make proper notecards and bibliographies.

Skills:

Making notecards	Summarizing
Preparing bibliographies	Neatness
Collecting data	Spelling
Handwriting	Organizing

Handouts Provided:

- Student Research Guide (see Appendix)
  a. "Bibliographies"
  b. "Notecards and Bibliographies"

PROJECT CALENDAR:

HOUR 1: _____	HOUR 2: _____	HOUR 3: _____
Discussion about notecards and bibliography cards, using the Student Research Guide for reference. Examples are done in class. HANDOUTS PROVIDED PREPARATION REQUIRED STUDENTS TURN IN WORK	Discussion about common mistakes made on notecards turned in at the end of Hour 1. Students are asked to correctly place information on an overhead transparency showing notecards and bibliography cards. RETURN STUDENT WORK PREPARATION REQUIRED	
HOUR 4: _____	HOUR 5: _____	HOUR 6: _____
HOUR 7: _____	HOUR 8: _____	HOUR 9: _____

Lesson Plans and Notes

HOUR 1: Tell students to open their research guides to the page titled "Notecards and Bibliographies." Spend a few minutes explaining this handout before the following activity takes place.

Read certain facts to the students from a variety of sources that you supply. As a class, in a step-by-step manner, the students should record these facts on notecards and make bibliography cards for each source. The handout discussed at the beginning of class is used by students as a reference throughout the hour. The cards are handed in at the end of the hour to be graded. For example, if oceanography is your topic, the first part of the hour could go something like this:

Teacher says...	Students write...
"First we will make a proper notecard. As the course is Oceanography, the heading 'Oceanography' goes at the top of your card."	"Oceanography" (at the top of their first notecard)
"The topic is whales."	"Whales" (on the next line)
"Here is the information for your body of the card: 'Whales range in length from 4 to 100 feet and can weigh from 160 pounds to 150 tons!'"	"Whales range in length from 4 to 100 feet and can weigh from 160 pounds to 150 tons."
"Now make a bibliography card showing where you found the information you just recorded. Begin with the heading 'Oceanography.'"	"Oceanography"
"Next, write 'Topic: Whales' on the line below."	"Topic: Whales"
This is our first source so label it 'Bibliography Card no. 1.' You may abbreviate the words. This goes on the same line as the topic."	"Bib. card no. 1"
"Our information on whales came from a one-volume encyclopedia written by Jacques Cousteau and his staff. The name of the person who wrote this source is the next piece of information we record, so write 'Author: Cousteau, Jacques,	

and staff" two lines below "Topic: Whales.'"

"The title of the article is 'Large Things to Save.'"

"The name of the encyclopedia is *The Cousteau Almanac.*"

"The date of publication is 1981."

"Since we are recording this source as an encyclopedia and not as a book, we must record its volume number. Write 'Volume: I (one-volume encyclopedia).'"

"The information was found on page 286."

"To show on your *notecard* where the information came from, write 'see bib. card no. 1' at the bottom of the first card we did."

"Author: Cousteau, Jacques, and staff"

"Title: Large Things to Save"

"Encyclopedia: *The Cousteau Almanac*"

"Date of Publication: (1981)"

"Volume: I (one-volume encyclopedia)"

"Page: 286"

"see bib. card no. 1"

Continue this process until students have recorded a number of notecards cross-referenced with bibliography cards, all about oceanography. More than one fact should be recorded from each source so that there are more notecards than bibliography cards. Students hand in their cards at the end of the hour.

Notes:

- You must supply sources of information for Hour 1, and come to class with notecards and bibliographies that are ready to be presented. Choose a topic that fits in with something you are presently teaching.

- You may want to make transparencies of the examples that are provided with this project description. This is a simple way to show your students how notecards and bibliography cards should look.

HOUR 2: Hand back the graded notecards and bibliography cards to the students. Use a transparency to project a notecard and bibliography card on a screen while pointing out and explaining various mistakes and misunderstandings. Then ask the students to come to the overhead projector and correctly write a variety of facts and information on a second transparency that shows a blank notecard and a blank bibliography card. You may want to require students at their desks to record the same information on notecards. At the end of this hour most students should be able to use notecards and bibliography cards without much help. Discuss the usefulness of notecard skills in future projects.

Note:

- Make large blank notecards on posterboard or on the chalkboard instead of on overheads for this hour if you do not have a projector available.

Transparencies, however, are easiest to use if students are going to write on them. Come to class prepared with a number of notecard and bibliography examples that can be used for discussion and practice during the hour.

Notecard Example

```
┌─────────────────────────────────────────────────┐
│              OCEANOGRAPHY                         │
│  TOPIC: WHALES              CARD NO. 1            │
│                                                   │
│     WHALES RANGE IN SIZE FROM 4 TO                │
│  100 FEET AND FROM 160 POUNDS TO                  │
│  150 TONS.                                        │
│                                                   │
│                                                   │
│                                                   │
│               BIBLIOGRAPHY CARD NO. 1             │
│                                                   │
└─────────────────────────────────────────────────┘
```

Bibliography Card Example

```
┌─────────────────────────────────────────────────┐
│              OCEANOGRAPHY                         │
│  TOPIC: WHALES            BIB. CARD NO. 1         │
│                                                   │
│   AUTHOR: COUSTEAU, JACQUES, AND STAFF            │
│   TITLE: "LARGE THINGS TO SAVE"                   │
│   ENCYCLOPEDIA: THE COUSTEAU ALMANAC              │
│   DATE OF PUBLICATION: (1981)                     │
│   VOLUME: I (ONE-VOLUME ENCYCLOPEDIA)             │
│   PAGE: 286                                       │
│                                                   │
│                                                   │
└─────────────────────────────────────────────────┘
```

If the source were a *book* instead of an encyclopedia, the bibliography card should look like this:

Bibliography Card Example

```
┌─────────────────────────────────────────────────────┐
│          OCEANOGRAPHY                                 │
│  TOPIC: WHALES                    BIB. CARD NO. 1     │
│                                                       │
│   AUTHOR: COUSTEAU, JACQUES, AND STAFF                │
│   TITLE: THE COUSTEAU ALMANAC                         │
│   PLACE OF PUBLICATION: GARDEN CITY, NY               │
│   DATE OF PUBLICATION: 1981                           │
│   PUBLISHER: DOUBLEDAY AND CO.                        │
│   PAGE: 286                                           │
│                                                       │
│                                                       │
└─────────────────────────────────────────────────────┘
```

INFORMATION SEARCH

Teacher Preview

Length of Project: 1 hour
Goal: To increase students' research skills
Level of Independence: Basic

During This Project Students Will:

1. Be introduced to the various sources of general information available in their classroom, school, or public library.
2. Apply notecard and bibliography skills.
3. Demonstrate their ability to find information from general resources in a library.

Skills:

Making notecards	Organizing
Preparing bibliographies	Individualized study habits
Library skills	Summarizing
Collecting data	Spelling
Neatness	

Handouts Provided:

No handouts are needed for this project.

PROJECT CALENDAR:

HOUR 1: _____	HOUR 2: _____	HOUR 3: _____
Students search through various sources to find information about specific topics. Note-cards and bibliography cards are completed for each source. NEED SPECIAL MATERIALS PREPARATION REQUIRED STUDENTS TURN IN WORK		
HOUR 4: _____	HOUR 5: _____	HOUR 6: _____
HOUR 7: _____	HOUR 8: _____	HOUR 9: _____

Lesson Plans and Notes

HOUR 1: Before class, write each of the Information Search Topics provided with this project on a separate card. In class, each student takes one of these topics (blind draw!) and then finds at least two sources of information about it in the school library. General references are adequate for this project.

After properly heading notecards, students record three short quotes from each source they find. They also make one bibliography card for each source. Notecards must have references to bibliography card numbers because it is important to know the source of each quote. Students work with as many different topics as they can before handing in notecards and bibliography cards at the end of the hour.

The assignment you give at the beginning of the hour goes something like this:

1. The course title is "Library Skills," so head all notecards that way.
2. Record the topic from the card you choose on the second line of each notecard.
3. Complete these things for *each* topic you work with:
   a. Find two different sources of information.
   b. Find three short quotes from each of these sources (six quotes in all).
   c. Record each quote on a separate notecard.
   d. Number your notecards correctly.
   e. Make a bibliography card for each source and number these cards.
   f. On each notecard make a reference to the bibliography card which tells the source of the quote.

Notes:

• Instead of using this project only once, you may prefer to do it in three one-hour steps as you teach library skills:
   a. In a classroom with encyclopedias and other general references
   b. In a school library
   c. In a public library

• Be sure your students know how to locate various sources of information in the library before having them do this project. For simplicity, primary emphasis should be placed on general references like encyclopedias and almanacs.

• Observe your students' ability to work on their own during this project. Use it as an opportunity to emphasize and evaluate independent learning.

• Instead of writing out each topic yourself before class, you can assign each student a topic from the list provided at the beginning of the hour.

• This project may be used to emphasize more advanced library skills, particularly if you have access to a public library. Require students to use the card catalog, computer catalog, and *Readers' Guide to Periodical Literature* as well as general references. Increase the number of required sources for each topic from two to three or four.

Information Search Topics

electricity	geometry	France
boa constrictor	pepper	England
corn	salt	China
gardens	maple tree	Battle of the Bulge
Martin Luther King, Jr.	Henry Ford	zebra
Eleanor Roosevelt	Golda Meir	x-rays
windmills	Booker T. Washington	worms
grasshoppers	osmosis	architecture
carnivores	oxygen	botany
geology	nitrogen	George Washington Carver
Paris	herbivore	Thomas Edison
the moon	vertebrate	Marie Curie
sunflowers	petroleum	irrigation
Napoleon Bonaparte	lightning	fertilizer
Joan of Arc	dogs	Wyoming
Frederick Douglass	cats	pollination
solar energy	reptiles	skeleton
arithmetic	birds	arboreal
geography	amphibians	dolphin
Asia	fish	wolf
Europe	Davy Crockett	white-tailed deer
Africa	Martha Washington	rabbit
America	A. Philip Randolph	octopus
Australia	deciduous trees	blood
teeth	water buffalo	eye
weaving	kangaroo	camouflage
beans	poison ivy	African lion
trigonometry	London	raccoon
algebra	Iran	John F. Kennedy
oak tree	mammals	Vincent Van Gogh
xylophone	jazz	sculpture

LIBRARY PROJECT

Teacher Preview

Length of Project: 5 hours
Goal: To increase students' research skills
Level of Independence: Basic

During This Project Students Will:

1. Gain experience in locating and recording information from library resources.
2. Decide or make deductions about which source to use for answers to specific questions.
3. Review their work and discuss how it may apply to future projects.

Skills:

Individualized study habits   Preparing bibliographies
Library skills   Making notecards
Summarizing   Neatness
Handwriting
Individualized study habits

Handouts Provided:

- Teacher's Introduction to the Student Research Guide (Optional; see Appendix)
  a. "Typical Library Quiz"

- Student Research Guide (see Appendix)
  a. "Dewey Decimal Classification System"
  b. "The Card Catalog"
  c. *"Readers' Guide to Periodical Literature"*

- "Library Activity 1"
- "Library Activity 2"
- "Library Activity 3"

PROJECT CALENDAR:

HOUR 1: _____	HOUR 2: _____	HOUR 3: _____
Discussion of the library and what it has to offer. Class review of general references, card catalogs, and *Readers' Guide to Periodical Literature*.	Students do Activity 1 in the library.	Students do Activity 2 in the library.
HANDOUTS PROVIDED	HANDOUT PROVIDED STUDENTS TURN IN WORK	HANDOUT PROVIDED STUDENTS TURN IN WORK
HOUR 4: _____	**HOUR 5:** _____	**HOUR 6:** _____
Students do Activity 3 in the library.	Review of student work on each of the three activities. Mistakes are discussed and questions are answered. The usefulness of library skills is pointed out. Optional: Library Quiz.	
HANDOUT PROVIDED STUDENTS TURN IN WORK	RETURN STUDENT WORK	
HOUR 7: _____	**HOUR 8:** _____	**HOUR 9:** _____

Lesson Plans and Notes

HOUR 1: Spend this hour discussing the various areas of the library and what kinds of things can be found in each. Use handouts from the Student Research Guide to review the card catalog, the Dewey Decimal Classification System, and the *Readers' Guide to Periodical Literature*. Explain what each of the three library activities will require:

Activity 1—Students use *only* general references, primarily encyclopedias, to answer questions on a handout.

Activity 2—Students use *only* the card catalog to answer questions on a handout.

Activity 3—Students use the entire library to answer questions on a handout.

Note:

• If your students have no library training or experience, an additional hour may be necessary to prepare them for this project. Perhaps a preliminary trip to the library for instruction from a trained librarian and a tour of the library would help set the stage.

HOUR 2: Give students the handout for "Library Activity 1" and have them spend the hour conducting research in encyclopedias and other general references. This activity can take place in a fairly confined area of the library or even in a classroom if enough reference materials are available (three sets of encyclopedias, *minimum.)* Students hand their work in at the end of the hour.

Notes:

• Activities 1 and 2 are designed for students to work on individually, but they can also be used with pairs or small groups of three or four students each.

• Encourage (or even assign!) students to start working at different places on the worksheet, to avoid having 30 people scrambling for the answer to the first question at the same time.

HOUR 3: Give students the handout for "Library Activity 2" and have them spend the hour conducting research in the card catalog. This must take place in a library. Students hand their work in at the end of the hour.

Notes:

• It is a good idea to notify the library of a planned visit and discuss the project with a librarian.

• An additional activity is to return to the library and have students trade papers and check each other's answers for questions 19–25. This gives students another opportunity to work with the card catalog. There may be several correct answers for every question. Those students who cannot verify an answer can write a note and you can check it later (or check it right then if time permits.)

HOUR 4: Give students the handout for "Library Activity 3" and spend the hour conducting research throughout the library. Students work in pairs. Partners should be identified before the hour begins. Students hand their work in at the end of the hour.

Notes:

- The questions in Sets II and III of Activity 3 require students to find books and other resources in the library. Students should understand that some books may not be on the shelves for one reason or another. If a book isn't on the shelf there is no option but to choose another question to work on.

- You should make a student answer sheet for Activity 3 so that their answers are organized. A useful answer sheet consists of three pages labeled "Set I," "Set II," and "Set III," with a line for each answer.

- As with Activity 2, you can return to the library and have students grade their own (or someone else's) work. Allow partners to work together in checking answers.

HOUR 5: This hour is designed for discussion and review. Point out common mistakes that were made on the handouts and emphasize correct procedures for library research. A library quiz may be given. This is an excellent time to discuss the usefulness of research skills and how such skills are applied in high school, college, and various careers. Remind students that the goal of independent learning begins with the ability to find and record information.

General Notes for the Project:

- Each handout represents a one-hour activity that is designed to determine how proficient students are in the use of library skills. Students are not expected to finish a handout; they are required to complete as much work as possible in one hour.

- There are no answer sheets provided for these activities. Some questions have more than one possible answer and others have different answers for different libraries. In addition, it will be useful for you to find out what is available in *your* library. Record answers as students find them and they are verified by you or a librarian, and you will soon have a complete set for this project.

Name _____

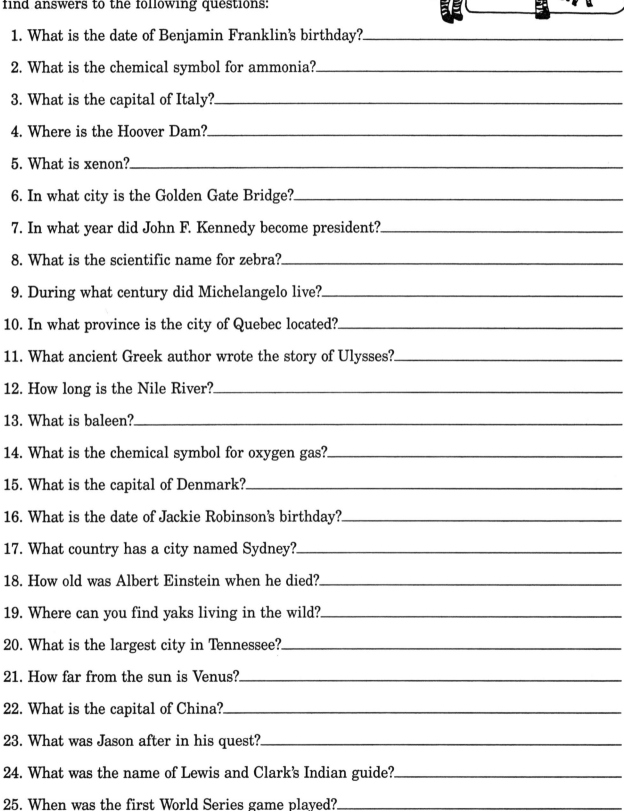

LIBRARY ACTIVITY 1

Using only encyclopedias and other general reference materials, find answers to the following questions:

1. What is the date of Benjamin Franklin's birthday?_____

2. What is the chemical symbol for ammonia?_____

3. What is the capital of Italy?_____

4. Where is the Hoover Dam?_____

5. What is xenon?_____

6. In what city is the Golden Gate Bridge?_____

7. In what year did John F. Kennedy become president?_____

8. What is the scientific name for zebra?_____

9. During what century did Michelangelo live?_____

10. In what province is the city of Quebec located?_____

11. What ancient Greek author wrote the story of Ulysses?_____

12. How long is the Nile River?_____

13. What is baleen?_____

14. What is the chemical symbol for oxygen gas?_____

15. What is the capital of Denmark?_____

16. What is the date of Jackie Robinson's birthday?_____

17. What country has a city named Sydney?_____

18. How old was Albert Einstein when he died?_____

19. Where can you find yaks living in the wild?_____

20. What is the largest city in Tennessee?_____

21. How far from the sun is Venus?_____

22. What is the capital of China?_____

23. What was Jason after in his quest?_____

24. What was the name of Lewis and Clark's Indian guide?_____

25. When was the first World Series game played?_____

Name _____ Date _____

LIBRARY ACTIVITY 2

Using only the card catalog, answer these questions:

1. Who wrote *The Pickwick Papers?*_____

2. Who wrote *Gone with the Wind?*_____

3. Name one book written by Daniel Defoe._____

4. What is the call number for *Moby Dick?*_____

5. Does your library have the *Complete Works of Shakespeare?*_____

6. How many pages are in *Don Quixote?*_____

7. What is the publication date of *The Hobbit?*_____

8. In what year was George Orwell born?_____

9. What is the call number for *The Grapes of Wrath?*_____

10. What is one book written by T.H. White?_____

11. What is the call number for *The Iliad?*_____

12. When was C.S. Lewis born?_____

13. What is the publication date for *A Tale of Two Cities?*_____

14. Who wrote *Native Son?*_____

15. How many pages are in *Anna Karenina?*_____

16. Name one book written by Leon Uris._____

17. How many books by John Barth are in your library?_____

18. Name one book written by Kurt Vonnegut, Jr._____

On a separate piece of paper, record:

19. The author and title of any book about astronomy.
20. The author and title of any book about elephants.
21. The author and title of any book about computers.
22. The author and title of any book about railroads.
23. The author and title of any book about jewelry.
24. The author and title of any book about zebras.
25. The author and title of any book about yachting.

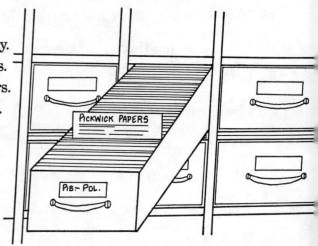

Name _____ Date _____

LIBRARY ACTIVITY 3

Partner's Name 1._____

2._____

This project is not a test. It is designed to let you and your partner make use of the library skills you have learned. The more adept you are at using the library the more points you will be able to accumulate. The goal of this project is to earn as many points as possible by working cooperatively with your partner. For this activity you may use the entire library to find information.

There are three sets of questions on this handout. The questions are divided according to their difficulty: Set I contains the easiest questions, Set II questions are harder to answer, and Set III are made up of the most difficult questions in the activity. Before starting this activity, you and your partner must decide which questions to answer, because it is not possible to answer them all. Set I questions are worth *one point* each; Set II questions are worth *three points*, each, and Set III questions are worth *five points* each. This means that you and your partner should plan how to accumulate the most points in the time allowed.

You will be told how much time you have to search the library for answers. At the end of the time you will hand in your answer sheet. You will be given points for *correct answers only*.

SET I QUESTIONS
(1 point each)

1. Who wrote *Les Misérables*?

2. From what state was Thomas Jefferson?

3. When was John Steinbeck born?

4. What is the speed of light?

5. In what state is Mount Rushmore?

6. What is the call number for *A Tale of Two Cities*?

7. How many pages are in *Huckleberry Finn*?

8. What kind of a wind is a zephyr?

9. What is the capital of Wyoming?

10. In what continent is the Amazon River?

11. Name one book written by Alex Haley.

12. When is Martin Luther King, Jr.'s birthday?

13. Who was Alexander the Great's father?

14. What city is at the mouth of the Mississippi River?

15. What is the call number for *I, Claudius*?

16. When was Jules Verne born?

17. When did Benjamin Franklin die?

18. Who wrote *A Farewell to Arms*?

19. What is the chemical symbol for iron?

20. Where did George Washington Carver teach?

21. What state has a city called Saint Paul?

22. In what state is Yosemite National Park?

23. What is the call number for *Catch-22*?

24. What is the capital of Pakistan?

25. Who wrote *Absalom, Absalom!*?

SET II QUESTIONS
(3 points each)

1. Who wrote *War and Peace*? Into how many books is this story divided? On what page does "Book II" begin?

2. Who wrote *A Tale of Two Cities*? What are the first twelve words of this story? Into how many books is this story divided?

3. Who wrote *Of Mice and Men*? What river is mentioned in the first sentence of the book? How many chapters are in this book?

4. Who wrote *Gulliver's Travels*? Into how many parts is the book divided? What is the first sentence of this story?

5. Who wrote *The Red Badge of Courage*? In the first sentence, what was "stretched out over the hills, resting"? Into how many chapters is this book divided?

For questions 6, 7, 8, 9, and 10, find one book for each topic (you may *not* use encyclopedias!) and record the title of the book and the author's name. Then record one simple fact from each book. Tell what pages you find your facts on.

6. Grasshoppers: book title, author, fact, page

7. Ballet: book title, author, fact, page

8. Earthquakes: book title, author, fact, page

9. Automobiles: book title, author, fact, page

10. Democracy: book title, author, fact, page

For questions 11, 12, 13, 14, and 15, find one book *about each person* you named (you may *not* use encyclopedias!) and record the title of the book and the author's name. Then record one simple fact from each book. Tell what pages you find your facts on. Remember, you are looking for biographies and autobiographies here.

11. Queen Victoria (Queen of England): book title, author, fact, page

12. Frederick Douglass: book title, author, fact, page

13. Thomas Edison: book title, author, fact, page

14. Adolf Hitler: book title, author, fact, page

15. Golda Meir: book title, author, fact, page

SET III QUESTIONS
(5 points each)

Find one source of information and make a complete bibliography for each topic. You must also make *two* notecards for each topic. The notecards must each contain one fact and be properly made. See your Student Research Guide for the correct method of making bibliographies and notecards.

1. The current prime minister of Israel: bibliography and two notecards.

2. The current president of the United States: bibliography and two notecards.

3. The current premier of the Soviet Union: bibliography and two notecards.

4. Solar eclipses: bibliography and two notecards.

5. Acid rain: bibliography and two notecards.

LETTER WRITING

Teacher Preview

Length of Project: 3 hours
Goal: To increase students' research skills
Level of Independence: Basic

During This Project Students Will:

1. Be shown how to write a letter requesting information.
2. Compose a "practice" business letter.
3. Write a formal letter to a business, organization, or individual of their choice, which asks for specific information.
4. Analyze the information they receive from answered requests.

Skills:

Writing letters	Paragraphs
Handwriting	Spelling
Grammar	Neatness
Sentences	

Handouts Provided:

- Student Research Guide (see Appendix)
  a. "Sending for Information"
  b. "Example of the 'Block Letter' Style"
  c. "Example of a 'Modified Block Letter' Style"

PROJECT CALENDAR:

HOUR 1: _____	HOUR 2: _____	HOUR 3: _____
Discussion of business letters. Students write letters to one specific address, asking for information. The letters are not sent.	Students search for addresses and write letters requesting information. After being checked, the letters are sent.	Several weeks or months after Hour 2, students read and critically evaluate letter responses in class.
PREPARATION REQUIRED HANDOUTS PROVIDED STUDENTS TURN IN WORK	PREPARATION REQUIRED STUDENTS TURN IN WORK NEED SPECIAL MATERIALS	
HOUR 4: _____	HOUR 5: _____	HOUR 6: _____
HOUR 7: _____	HOUR 8: _____	HOUR 9: _____

Lesson Plans and Notes

HOUR 1: Each student in the class writes a letter to the same address asking for information. The hour begins with an introduction to the parts of a business letter. Use the "Sending for Information" handout from the Student Research Guide for reference and discussion. Examples of letter styles can also be found there.

Then, with the pertinent information about an organization written on the chalkboard (address, type of organization, person to contact, kinds of information available, and so forth), the class discusses what should be included in a letter to that particular place, asking for a specific type of information. Finally, each student composes a letter which is handed in at the end of the hour. These letters are graded but never sent.

Notes:

- An additional hour may be needed for this project if you intend to spend much time on the mechanics of letter writing.
- Come to class prepared with the address of an institution, organization, government office, or place of business that can be used by everyone for this activity; for example, the National Zoo in Washington, D.C. Put the address on the board and discuss what kinds of information might be available from this source. Allow students to decide for themselves what specific information to ask for in their letters.

HOUR 2: Provide magazines, journals, pamphlets, brochures, government publications, business cards, telephone books (Yellow Pages), or other address sources in the classroom. Students may also bring sources from home. Each student chooses an address that might provide useful information, and writes a formal letter to that business, organization, group, or individual. These letters are turned in at the end of the hour with properly addressed envelopes. Those with mistakes are returned to students and become homework assignments to be rewritten and turned back in. Those without mistakes are sent.

Notes:

- Have arrangements made for stamps and envelopes to be available this hour.
- Providing a variety of address sources is important; the more the better so that students have some real choice about places to write.
- Be sure students stress their desire for *free* material in the letters they send.
- It is important that the school's address be used for a mailing address. This will prevent follow-up mailings and junk mail from being sent to the families of your students. Some places that send free material sell addresses to mass-mailing services.

- Explain during this hour that information received through the mail is often biased in favor of the person or group that sends it out. Students will have an opportunity in Hour 3 to critically examine what they receive.
- Have students think of ways to use information they will receive. If this project is used to do research in a specialized subject area such as "Environmental Pollution," for example, then they may want to start an information file and compile a "Class Report" on the subject.
- To create a bulletin board at the end of this project, have each student make a copy of his or her letter before it is sent. After Hour 3 students display the letters they sent next to the ones they received in response.

HOUR 3: Students bring their letter responses to class. This happens at least 4 to 8 weeks following Hour 2. These letters are read in class and analyzed for three things:

What is the letter style?

Is the letter biased or manipulative?

Is the information helpful or worth receiving?

USING THE TELEPHONE

Teacher Preview

Length of Project: 3 hours

Goal: To increase students' research skills

Level of Independence: Basic

During This Project Students Will:

1. Learn techniques for requesting information over the phone.
2. Begin to overcome apprehensions about using the telephone to gather information.
3. Demonstrate their ability to work on a project away from the classroom, on their own time.
4. Be introduced indirectly to the study of family budgets and economics.

Skills:

Individualized study habits	Listening
Collecting data	Handwriting
Individualized study habits	

Handouts Provided:

- "Budget Items"
- "Telephone Work Sheet"
- "Family Budget Chart"

PROJECT CALENDAR:

HOUR 1: _____	HOUR 2: _____	HOUR 3: _____
Discussion about using the telephone to ask for information. Students role-play making phone calls.	Introduction to the project: students are assigned budget items and items are discussed. Review telephone manners. HANDOUTS PROVIDED	Discussion of the information gathered by students. Data are recorded on a chart. HANDOUT PROVIDED
HOUR 4: _____	**HOUR 5:** _____	**HOUR 6:** _____
HOUR 7: _____	**HOUR 8:** _____	**HOUR 9:** _____

Lesson Plans and Notes

HOUR 1: Spend the first hour discussing how people use the phone to find answers to their questions and, more important, the proper method of asking someone for information over the telephone. Spend most of the hour on telephone manners. Each call that students make for this project should include these things:

1. Introduction
2. Explanation of the assignment
3. Respectful inquiry: "Do you mind if I ask you a few simple questions?"
4. Sincere thank you (even if the person declines to answer questions)

The last part of the hour is used for role-playing, with students "calling" each other (one at a time!) while the rest of the class critiques the caller's methods.

HOUR 2: Explain the telephone assignment. This project requires students to gather information that will be used to construct a family budget. Distribute the "Budget Items" handout and either assign or allow each student to select one of the items from it. The students' homework assignment is to telephone three different people and find out how much it costs to pay for their part of the budget. The handout lists items for a class of 30, if each student is responsible for one item and each item is used twice. By allowing more than one student to pursue the same item, interesting comparisons can be made.

Give students the "Telephone Work Sheet" handout to keep track of their calls and set a due date for Hour 3 when all results will be charted.

Notes:

- Students should talk to their parents before making calls, especially those students who are required to telephone two or three of their parents' friends. A note from you about this project can be sent home with the students if you think it is necessary.

- Discuss the kinds of questions that may be asked by the people who are called. There may be options or variables that affect how much something costs. Students should be instructed to ask for the least complicated option: the option that is most straightforward and that has the fewest "frills."

- Review telephone techniques and manners during this hour.

- Some of the items may need to be changed to suit your particular situation. Item 6, for example, asks for the cost of natural gas. If your community does not use natural gas, this can be changed to electricity, coal, or wood. Item 11, as another example, asks students to call three different travel agents. This item would require expensive long distance calls if you live in a small town or rural area. Read over each item before reproducing the handout and change the ones that would be difficult for the students in your area to complete.

• It is obvious that students could get answers to many of the items without making telephone calls. For this reason it is helpful to involve parents in the project. If they know when the project is being conducted and what its requirements are, you can be more certain that calls are being made.

HOUR 3: Students bring their completed "Telephone Work Sheet" handout to class and are given the "Family Budget Chart" handout. Students present the data they collected over the phone for budget items and fill in their charts with the amounts given. The discussion that ensues centers around using the telephone to gather information: difficulties, problems, successes, techniques, interesting stories, and questions. You may want to add an hour to discuss family budgets and handling money.

Note:

• This project can be greatly expanded by making use of the information that is charted. Understanding how much "necessities" cost can give students insight into family budgeting. It is very possible that the money from a $40,000 income that remains after taxes will not be sufficient to cover the expense of all 15 items. This presents an excellent opportunity for the class to do some real "family budgeting." This project, then, can be transformed into an economics class.

General Note About This Project:

• A telephone should be available at school for students who do not have access to one at home.

BUDGET ITEMS

This project is designed to let you use the telephone to conduct research. The phone is a powerful research tool. It allows you to reach knowledgeable people who can help you answer questions or solve problems. As with all research skills, using the telephone is something you get better at with practice. Remember, the purpose of projects like this one is to help you become more comfortable with a tool that you undoubtedly will use more and more as you get older.

Your assignment is to become a member of an imaginary family of four with a total income of $40,000. Make three phone calls for the budget item you are assigned and use the "Telephone Worksheet" to record your questions and responses.

1. Your family must buy a new car. Decide what kind of car you want to buy (talk it over with your parents!), and then call a dealer to find out how much this car will cost without a trade-in. Use your own judgment about options such as air conditioning and automatic transmission. Ask the dealer to quote you a price of a car that is actually on the lot. Also, call a bank and a savings-and-loan association to find out how much your monthly payments on this car would be if you make a $2,000 down payment. How long will you have to make these payments?

2. Your family must buy clothes. The cost of clothing can vary greatly for different families, but you must get a rough idea by calling three of your parents' friends and asking them to give you an *estimate* of how much money they think a family of four might spend on clothing in one year. Tell them your class family has an income of $40,000.

3. You decide to buy health insurance for you and your family. Call an insurance agent and ask what the monthly premium would be for comprehensive health insurance policy for a family of four. Call two more agents (who represent different companies) to compare premium costs.

4. You and your family decide that it is time to buy a new house. You have saved $10,000 for a down payment and your total family (four people) income is $40,000 per year. Call three real estate agents and find out what the most expensive home you can afford will cost. What will the monthly payments be? Tell the real estate agents that your family has no major debts.

5. Your old car needs a tune-up, a complete lubrication, and all of the filters changed. Call three different garages or mechanic shops to find out how much this will cost. Be ready to tell them what kind of car you have.

6. You heat your home, heat your water, and cook with natural gas. During a typical year, you use an *average* of 200 CCF (CCF = 100 cubic feet) of gas per month. Call your gas company to find out how much your monthly bill should be. Call two of your parents' friends and ask them how much they pay per month for natural gas.

7. Your family uses electricity at an average rate of 1200 kilowatt hours per month. Call your local electric company and ask how much your monthly bill would be. Call two of your parents' friends and ask them how many kilowatt hours of electricity they use per month and what their monthly bills are.

8. You decide to buy a life insurance policy for yourself. Call an insurance agent and ask what the monthly premium for a $100,000 life insurance policy would be for a person your age and a person 30 years old. Call two more agents (who represent different companies) to compare premium costs.

9. Call the telephone company and ask how much their most basic, no-frills *local* service will cost per month if you own your own telephones. Call two of your parents' friends and ask them what their monthly bills for *local* service are.

10. Find out how much your family spends per week on groceries. Call three friends of your parents who have families of four or more people. Ask them how much they spend per week for food on the average. An educated guess is close enough. Be sure to record the size of each family you call.

11. Your family will take a two-week vacation this summer, either to Disneyland in California or Walt Disney World in Florida. Choose one place and call three different travel agents to find out how much it will cost to take a family of four there for two weeks. This will include transportation and lodging, but not food.

12. Your family must pay income taxes. Call the appropriate offices or departments or people to find out how much federal, state, and local income taxes will be for a family of four (four exemptions) with a gross income of $40,000 (husband and wife filing a joint return). Assume there are no other deductions. Also, when you call about federal taxes, you must find out how much money you will have to pay to social security (FICA).

13. Your family will take a two-week camping trip to a park in your home state. Choose two state parks and a federal park (or forest), and call the proper state and federal departments, or a tourist bureau, travel agent, or other person who would know, to find out how much it will cost to camp in each park for two weeks.

14. Your family must pay for water and sewage services from the city. Call the appropriate city department to find out how much city sewage rates are and how much city water costs per hundred cubic feet. Call two of your parents' friends and ask how much water their families use in one year (in hundred cubic feet), *or* ask them how much they pay per year in water bills.

15. Your family must pay property taxes. Call three of your parents' friends who own their homes and ask them how much they pay per year in property taxes.

© 1987 by The Center for Applied Research in Education, Inc.

ONLY!!
$150 Down
$250 per month

Name _____ Date _____

TELEPHONE WORK SHEET

Use this handout to help record data when you telephone for information about budget items.

ASSIGNED BUDGET ITEM NO.____:

_____

Write an introductory paragraph to use when you begin your phone call.

_____

_____

First Call to: _____

QUESTIONS	RESPONSES
1. _____	1. _____
2. _____	2. _____
3. _____	3. _____

Second Call to: _____

QUESTIONS	RESPONSES
1. _____	1. _____
2. _____	2. _____
3. _____	3. _____

Third Call to: _____

QUESTIONS	RESPONSES
1. _____	1. _____
2. _____	2. _____
3. _____	3. _____

Use a second sheet of paper if your questions or responses won't fit on this handout. Be prepared to explain these responses in class.

FAMILY BUDGET CHART

Use this chart to record data collected over the phone by your classmates for each budget item. You will end up with two sets of figures if two students researched the same item, so space is provided on the chart for each set of answers.

ITEM 1: NEW CAR

Price	Bank: Monthly Payment	Savings and Loan Monthly Payment

ITEM 2: CLOTHING

Friend 1	Friend 2	Friend 3

ITEM 3: HEALTH INSURANCE

Agent 1	Agent 2	Agent 3

ITEM 4: NEW HOUSE

Realtor 1		Realtor 2		Realtor 3	
Cost	Monthly Payment	Cost	Monthly Payment	Cost	Monthly Payment

ITEM 5: CAR MAINTENANCE

Garage 1	Garage 2	Garage 3

ITEM 6: NATURAL GAS

Gas Company	Friend 1	Friend 2

ITEM 7: ELECTRICITY

Electric Company	Friend 1	Friend 2

ITEM 8: LIFE INSURANCE

Agent 1		Agent 2		Agent 3	
Your Premium	30 Years Old	Your Premium	30 Years Old	Your Premium	30 Years Old

ITEM 9: TELEPHONE

Telephone Company	Friend 1	Friend 2

ITEM 10: FOOD/GROCERIES

Friend 1	Friend 2	Friend 3

ITEM 11: VACATION (TRAVEL)

Agent 1	Agent 2	Agent 3

ITEM 12: INCOME TAXES

Federal		State Taxes	Local Taxes
FICA*	Taxes		

ITEM 13: VACATION (CAMPING)

State Park 1	State Park 2	Federal Park 3

ITEM 14: WATER/SEWAGE

City	Friend 1	Friend 2

ITEM 15: PROPERTY TAXES

Friend 1	Friend 2	Friend 3

*Social Security

© 1987 by The Center for Applied Research in Education, Inc.

R-6

RESEARCH PROJECTS

Teacher Preview

Length of Each Project: 16 hours
Level of Independence: Intermediate
Four Research Categories:

American History
Native Americans
World History
The World of Science and Inventions

General Explanation: These four research projects are virtually identical in structure, with each offering a different subject area to study while requiring the use of a basic set of research and presentation skills. It is suggested that only one, or at most, two of them be used with a group of students in any given school year, to avoid repetition and potential boredom.

Goals:

1. To require the use of research skills as students learn about specific topics.
2. To emphasize independent learning.
3. To promote the concept of "kids teaching kids."

During This Project Students Will:

1. Define and select topics for research.
2. Combine the research skills they have mastered into one individualized project.
3. Assemble information for a report.
4. Present what they have learned to the rest of the class.
5. Discuss and analyze the project upon its completion.

Skills:

Preparing bibliographies	Persistence
Collecting data	Sentences
Making notecards	Sense of quality
Summarizing	Creating presentation strategies

Writing

Selecting topics

Following project outlines

Meeting deadlines

Accepting responsibility

Individualized study habits

Time-management

Personal motivation

Grammar

Paragraphs

Drawing and sketching

Poster making

Public speaking

Self-confidence

Teaching others

Neatness

Handwriting

Spelling

Divergent-convergent-evaluative thinking

Library Skills

Concentration

Controlling behavior

Handouts Provided:

- "Student Introduction to the Research Project"
- "Student Assignment Sheet" for each area of study
- Teacher's Introduction to the Student Research Guide (optional; see Appendix)
  a. "Notecard Evaluation"
  b. "Poster Evaluation"
  c. "Oral Presentation Evaluation"
- Student Research Guide (optional; see Appendix)
  a. "Choosing a Subject"
  b. "Audio-Visual and Written Information Guides"
  c. "Where to Go or Write for Information"
  d. "Project Fact Sheet"
  e. "Poster Display Sheet"
  f. "Things to Check Before Giving Your Presentation"
  g. "Visual Aids for the Oral Presentation"
  h. "Things to Remember When Presenting Your Project"
  i. "Daily Log"

PROJECT CALENDAR:

HOUR 1: _____	HOUR 2: _____	HOUR 3: _____
Discussion of the general requirements of a research project. Students are given their project assignment sheets.	(Optional): Discussion of checklists and evaluation forms from the Student Research Guide.	Students study in class from encyclopedias. Topic lists are begun.
HANDOUTS PROVIDED	HANDOUTS PROVIDED	
HOUR 4: _____	**HOUR 5: _____**	**HOUR 6: _____**
Students study in class from encyclopedias. Topic lists and final topic choices are turned in.	Final topic choices are returned with teacher approval. Students conduct research.	Students conduct research.
STUDENTS HAND IN WORK	RETURN STUDENT WORK	
HOUR 7: _____	**HOUR 8: _____**	**HOUR 9: _____**
Students conduct research.	Students conduct research. (Optional): Collect notecards and bibliographies at the end of the hour for a brief check.	Students begin working on posters and written reports.
		NEED SPECIAL MATERIALS

PROJECT CALENDAR:

HOUR 10: _____	HOUR 11: _____	HOUR 12: _____
Students work on posters and reports.	Work on posters and reports continues.	Students complete their work on posters and reports.
NEED SPECIAL MATERIALS	NEED SPECIAL MATERIALS	NEED SPECIAL MATERIALS
HOUR 13: _____	HOUR 14: _____	HOUR 15: _____
Students begin making presentations to the class.	Presentations to the class continue.	Finish presentations.
STUDENTS TURN IN WORK	STUDENTS TURN IN WORK	STUDENTS TURN IN WORK
HOUR 16: _____	HOUR 17: _____	HOUR 18: _____
Discussion about the skills used in this project: why they are important and how they could be used to study other things.		

Lesson Plans and Notes

HOUR 1: Give students the handout that introduces them to the general requirements of a research project. Most of the hour is discussion about what kinds of things research is used for and why it is important for a person to be able to find information, record it, put it into some kind of order, and present it to others. Point out that many careers require people to use these research skills and that certain skills are necessary regardless of what is being learned. Give students their assignment sheets during the last fifteen minutes of the hour and briefly discuss the requirements. The entire project will be explained during Hour 3.

HOUR 2: (Optional) Introduce students to the evaluation forms and student checklists that are provided in the Student Research Guide. Explain each form and teach students how to use the checklists to keep track of their own projects.

Note:

- There are a number of teaching aids in the Student Research Guide (Appendix) that may be useful. These materials are optional and are not necessary for the successful completion of the project. However, it is worth the effort to look them over, especially the student checklists and evaluation sheets for notecards, posters, and oral presentations. The "Daily Log" handout is an excellent way for students to keep track of their own progress during this project.

HOUR 3: Spend the first part of the hour discussing the assignment handout and answering student questions. For the rest of the hour, each student studies encyclopedias and other general references to begin compiling a list of topics that could be used for a research project. This list is to be completed by the end of the next hour.

HOUR 4: Students continue to work on their topic lists by studying encyclopedias. When a list is completed, the student identifies which topic he or she intends to pursue for the remainder of the project. These lists and final topic selections are handed in at the end of the hour.

Note:

- Each assignment sheet calls for students to make lists of topics that they would like to study; these lists are to be handed in. The reason for this requirement is to allow you some control over topic selection, primarily to help students avoid the trap of choosing topics that are too difficult, exotic, or obscure.

HOUR 5: Students have their final topic selections returned with your approval. If you consider a topic to be inappropriate, tell the student to meet with you and select another topic from his or her list. Students who receive approval begin their research projects, using sources that are available in the room or that they have provided themselves.

Note:

- For successful completion of these projects it is very important that many resources be available to students, either in a library or in the classroom.

HOURS 6, 7, and 8: Research continues. At the end of hour 8, students may be required to hand in notecards and bibliography cards for a brief check before beginning work on posters and written reports.

HOURS 9, 10, 11, and 12: Students work on posters and written reports. Materials for poster making need to be available all four hours: posterboard, markers, rulers, colored pencils, drawing paper, scissors, glue/paste, and whatever other tools and materials are needed. Establish some method for cleaning up each hour, such as assigning student aides each day to run a simple checkout system. Many students are not accustomed to picking up after themselves or may not think it matters. Taking care of materials, however, is an important self-discipline skill and should be strongly emphasized.

HOURS 13, 14, and 15: Students present their projects to the class as oral reports. They are graded for presentation skills as well as project content. Posters are displayed in the classroom and written reports are handed in.

Note:

- If time does not permit three hours for individual presentations, posters and written reports can be handed in at the end of Hour 12. "Kids teaching kids" is an interesting experience, however, and gets across the point that students can learn from one another as well as from a teacher.

HOUR 16: This final hour is provided to help students see the ultimate value of the project they have just completed. Discuss the skills that are necessary for conducting a research project, producing a poster, and making an oral report. Ask students if they have a different perspective from what they had during Hour 1 when research was discussed in general terms. Spend time explaining how students who have gone through the experience of a research project such as this are prepared to tackle projects that allow even more independence. Ask students to name some things they feel confident they could learn about if given an opportunity. This helps reinforce the idea that what was learned from the project can be applied to many other learning situations.

General Notes About This Project:

- To be most effective as an introduction to independent study, these projects should be conducted in the classroom so that student work habits can be observed and to ensure that help is available when necessary. The outline can be modified, however, to meet individual needs: homework can be given, the number of classroom hours can be reduced or increased, and the basic assignment can be altered.

- "American History" and "World History" can be used as an introduction to a group project ("That Was the Year"), which is described later in this book.

STUDENT INTRODUCTION TO
THE RESEARCH PROJECT

Learning about something on your own requires a great deal of independence and self-motivation. Choosing a topic to study, finding information about it, and then presenting what you've learned to others involve many skills. You are being given the responsibility of doing a research project because you already possess many *basic* research skills and because the experience of learning on your own teaches things a teacher cannot give in a lecture.

Keep in mind that the topic you will be studying is probably not something you will need to know about to be successful in life, but the skills used to complete this project will help you a great deal in future courses and possibly your career as well. You will gain experience in the following areas:

1. Finding sources of information about a topic you choose to study.
2. Making notecards and bibliography cards while doing research.
3. Organizing the information from notecards into a written report.
4. Creating an interesting way to teach the rest of the class about your topic.
5. Designing a visual display that is eye-catching, informative, and complementary to your oral presentation.
6. Working from an outline to complete the requirements.
7. Meeting deadlines on time by disciplining yourself to do work and not waiting for someone else to spoon-feed you instructions.
8. Managing your study time so that it doesn't get used up talking with friends about the latest movie, bothering others who are trying to work, or hesitating to start because you're not sure how to go about it.
9. Solving problems as they arise and changing plans if you need to.
10. Presenting your work to others.

The specific requirements of your research project are outlined on a separate handout so that you can see the entire plan and organize your work accordingly. Once you are able to complete an assignment like this one on your own, it is logical that you could choose almost any topic and go about studying it. All subjects cannot be taught in school, but this should not keep you from learning about those that are of special interest to you. Apply the skills presented in this project and learn on your own.

Name _____ Date _____

AMERICAN HISTORY
Student Assignment Sheet

The subject of this research project is the history of America from its discovery to the present. You will select a period of time to study, identify one specific event from that period, and conduct a research project about that topic. To begin, choose a time period from the following list:

1492–1700	1920–1940
1700–1770	1940–1950
1770–1800	1950–1960
1800–1850	1960–1970
1850–1870	1970–1980
1870–1900	1980–PRESENT
1900–1920	

After a time period is selected, follow this assignment outline to complete the project:

I. Study the time period (in encyclopedias and other general references) and identify *at least* ten topics that you would be interested in investigating further. This list of topics will be handed in.

II. From this list choose *one* topic that you want to study.

III. Use a variety of sources (at least five) for your research. No more than three of these can be encyclopedias.

IV. Carefully and accurately record a minimum of twenty facts about the topic on notecards.

V. Make a bibliography card for each source.

VI. Write a three- to four-page report after using your notecards to organize an outline. Writing skills will be carefully graded on this report.

VII. Make a presentation to the class about your topic. Design an interesting poster for this presentation that includes your twenty facts and any other information you want to show visually.

VIII. At the conclusion of your presentation turn in these things:

A. Written report (three to four pages)
B. Twenty notecards
C. Five bibliography cards (or a bibliography sheet)
D. Poster

Hints for Successfully Completing This Project:

1. The time period you choose will offer many topics to study. Don't let this overwhelm you; first, narrow down the possibilities by identifying the ten topics that you know are covered in resources available to you. This will take a little time, but it is a necessary step in choosing a topic to study.

2. As you make your final topic selection, keep these things in mind:

   a. The topic should be specific enough to make a short report possible. If the time period is 1850–1870, for example, don't choose "The Civil War" as your topic because it is too general. Instead, you might decide upon "Three Major Civil War Battles" or "The Generals of the Civil War." You can even be more specific: "The Battle of Gettysburg" or "General Robert E. Lee." The more focused your topic, the more precise and in-depth the research report will be.

   b. Be certain that you can find at least five sources of information about your topic.

   c. You will be required to teach some important facts from your research to the rest of the class. Choose a topic (and facts) that is understandable to you and that can be taught or explained to others.

3. Many of the handouts from the Student Research Guide will be helpful as you work on this project and prepare for your presentation. These can be used for reference as you make notecards, bibliographies, a poster, and a final presentation to the class.

NATIVE AMERICANS
Student Assignment Sheet

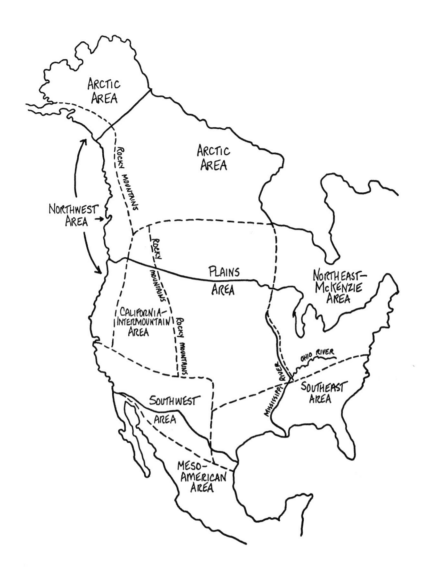

The subject of this research project is Indian tribes that are native to North America. You will select a tribe to study, identify one specific topic about that tribe, and conduct a research project about that topic. First, choose an Indian tribe from the following list, which is arranged according to "culture area":

    I. Meso-American area (southern Mexico and Central America)
       A. Maya   C. Aztec
       B. Toltec

    II. Southwestern area (northern Mexico and southwestern U.S.)
       A. Eastern Pueblos   C. Navaho
       B. Western Pueblos D. Apache

    III. Southeastern area (southeastern U.S. and extreme northeast Mexico)
       A. Choctaw   C. Cherokee
       B. Creek   D. Seminole

IV. Northeastern-McKenzie area (north of the Ohio River and Virginia, east of the Mississippi River, south of the arctic)

   A. Delaware   D. Fox
   B. Iroquois   E. Menomini
   C. Huron   F. Ojibwa

V. Plains area (from Texas northward into lower Canada)

   A. Blackfoot   D. Cheyenne
   B. Crow   E. Comanche
   C. Arapaho   F. Sioux

VI. California-Intermountain area (northwestern U.S., *excluding* coastal areas)

   A. Paiute   C. Nez Percé
   B. Shoshoni

VII. Northwest area (Pacific northwest, from central California to southern Alaska)

   A. Haidu   C. Nootka
   B. Bella Coola D. Chinook

VIII. Arctic area

   A. Alaskan Eskimo   C. Canadian Eskimo
   B. Aleut

After a tribe is selected, follow this assignment outline to complete the project.

I. Study the tribe (in encyclopedias and books about Indians) and identify *at least* five topics that you would be interested in investigating further. This list of topics will be handed in. Some examples of topics are:

   A. Dwellings   E. Religion
   B. Food   F. Warfare
   C. Furnishings and utensils   G. Art
   D. Clothing and ornaments   H. Language

II. From this list choose *one* topic that you want to study.

III. Use at least five different sources for your research. No more than three of these sources may be encyclopedias.

IV. Carefully and accurately record a minimum of twenty facts about the topic on notecards.

V. Make a bibliography card for each source.

VI. Write a three- to four-page report after using your notecards to create an outline. Writing skills will be graded carefully on this report.

VII. Make a presentation to the class about your topic. Design an interesting poster for this presentation that includes your twenty facts and any other information you want to show visually.

VIII. At the conclusion of your presentation, turn in these things:

   A. Written report (three to four pages)
   B. Twenty notecards
   C. Five bibliography cards (or a bibliography sheet)
   D. Poster

© 1987 by The Center for Applied Research in Education, Inc.

Hints for Successfully Completing This Project:

1. The Indian tribe you choose will offer many topics to study. Don't let this overwhelm you; first, narrow down the possibilities by identifying five topics that you know are covered in the resources available to you. This will take a little time, but it is a necessary step in choosing a topic to study.

2. As you make your final topic selection, keep these things in mind:

   a. The topic should be specific enough to make a short report possible. If your Indian tribe is the Nez Percé, for example, don't choose "The History of the Nez Percé" as your topic because it is too general. Instead, you might decide upon "Wars with White Men" or "The Chiefs of Nez Percé." You can be even more specific: "The Battle of September, 1877" or "Chief Joseph." The more focused your topic, the more precise and in-depth the research report will be.

   b. Be certain that you can find at least five sources of information about your topic.

   c. You will be required to teach some important facts about your topic to the rest of the class. Choose a topic that you understand and that can be taught or explained to others.

3. Many of the handouts from the Student Research Guide will be helpful as you work on this project and prepare for your presentation. They can be used for reference as you make notecards, bibliographies, a poster, and a final presentation to the class.

WORLD HISTORY
Student Assignment Sheet

The subject of this research project is the history of the world, from the beginning of recorded history to the present. You will select an area of the world from the list below, choose a time period from the history of that area, identify one specific topic from that period, and conduct a research project about it. First, choose an area from the following list:

Japan	Greece	U.S.S.R.
China	Rome/Italy	Poland
India	Israel	Northern Africa
Iran	France	Southern Africa
The Arab nations	Germany	Southeast Asia
Great Britain	Spain	
Australia	South America	

Any other area of the world (obtain your teacher's okay)

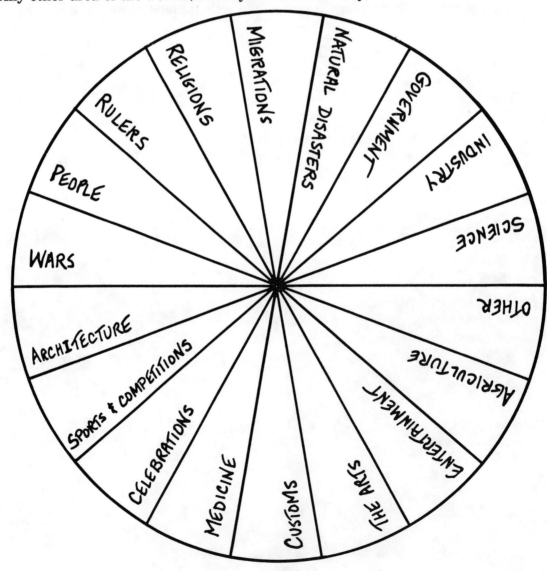

© 1997 by The Center for Applied Research in Education, Inc.

After you have selected an area of the world from the list above, follow this assignment outline to complete the project.

I. Study the area (in encyclopedias and other general references) and decide what general time period you want to learn more about. Some of the areas listed (such as Greece and the Middle East) have histories that go back several thousand years. Narrow your study down to a "brief" historical period. This may be as little as one week or as much as 50 to 100 years.

II. From this time period identify at least ten topics that you would be interested in investigating further (wars, people, rulers, religion, migrations, natural disasters, government, industry, science, agriculture, entertainment, the arts, and so forth). This list of topics and the time period you have chosen must be turned in.

III. From your list of topics choose *one* that you want to study for a research project.

IV. Locate at least five sources of information about this topic. No more than three of these sources may be encyclopedias.

V. Carefully and accurately record at least twenty facts about the topic on notecards.

VI. Make a bibliography card for each source.

VII. Write a three- to four-page report after using your notecards to create an outline. Writing skills will be graded carefully on this report.

VIII. Make a presentation to the class about your topic. Design an interesting poster for this presentation that includes your twenty facts and any other information you want to show visually.

IX. At the conclusion of your presentation turn in these things:
   A. Written report (three to four pages)
   B. Twenty notecards
   C. Five bibliography cards (or a bibliography sheet)
   D. Poster

Hints for Successfully Completing This Project:

1. When you choose a time period you are opening the door to a huge number of topics. Don't let this overwhelm you. First, narrow down the possibilities by identifying ten topics that you know have enough information available for good research topics. This will take a little time, but it is a necessary step in choosing a topic to study.

2. As you make your final topic selection, keep these things in mind:
   a. The topic should be specific enough to make a report possible. If you decide to study Rome during the fourth century A.D., for example, you should not choose "The Roman Empire" as your topic because it is too general. Instead, you might decide upon "Major Fourth-Century Wars" or "Emperors of the Fourth Century." You can be even more specific: "The Emperor Constantine." The more focused you can be with your topic, the more precise and in-depth the research report will be.
   b. Be certain that you can find at least five sources of information about the topic.
   c. You will be required to teach some important facts about your topic to the rest of the class. Choose a topic that is understandable to you and that can be taught or explained to others.

3. Many of the handouts from the Student Research Guide will be helpful as you work on this project. These can be used for reference as you make notecards, bibliographies, a poster, and a final presentation to the class.

47

Name _____ Date _____

THE WORLD OF SCIENCE AND INVENTIONS
Student Assignment Sheet

The subject of this research project is the world of science and inventions. You will select a general subject area, identify one specific topic from that area, and conduct a research project about it. First, choose a subject area from the following list:

Scientists and inventors   Oceanography
Geology   Archaeology
Chemistry   Physics
Animals in the wild   Entomology (insects)
Astronomy   Botany
Electricity   Zoology
Machines   Communications
Medicine   Transportation
Computers   Meteorology (weather)
Robotics   Light

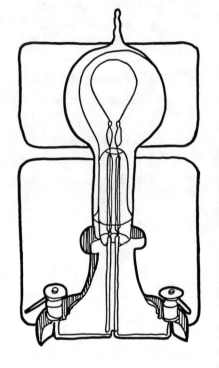

After you have selected a subject area, follow this assignment outline to complete the project.

I. Study the subject area (in encyclopedias and other general references) and identify *at least* ten topics that you would be interested in pursuing further. This list of topics must be handed in.

II. From your list choose *one* topic to study for a research project.

III. Locate at least five sources of information about your topic. No more than three of these sources can be encyclopedias.

IV. Carefully and accurately record at least twenty facts about this topic on notecards.

V. Make a bibliography card for each source.

VI. Write a three- to four-page report after arranging your notecards into an outline. Writing skills will be graded carefully on this report.

VII. Make a presentation to the class about your topic. For this presentation, make a poster that includes the twenty facts and any other information you want to show visually.

VIII. At the conclusion of your presentation turn in these things:

A. Written report (three to four pages)
B. Twenty notecards
C. Five bibliography cards (or a bibliography sheet)
D. Poster

Hints for Successfully Completing This Project:

1. When you choose a subject area you are opening the door to a huge number of topics. Don't let this overwhelm you; first, narrow the possibilities by identifying ten topics that you know have enough information available for good research projects. This will take a little time but it is a necessary step in choosing a topic to study.

2. As you make your final topic selection keep these things in mind:

   a. The topic should be specific enough to make a short report possible. If the subject area is zoology, for example, you should not choose "warm-blooded animals" as your topic because it is too general. Instead, you might decide upon "primates" or "flightless birds." You can be even more specific: "chimpanzee" or "ostrich." The more focused your topic, the more precise and in-depth your research project will be.

   b. Be certain that you can find at least five sources of information about your topic.

   c. You will be required to teach some important facts about your topic to the rest of the class. Be sure to choose a topic that is understandable to you and that can be taught or explained to others.

3. Many of the handouts from the Student Research Guide will be helpful as you work on this project. These can be used for reference as you make your notecards, bibliographies, a poster and a final presentation to the class.

OPENINGS

Teacher Preview

Length of Project: 2 hours for introduction, then 15 minutes per day

Level of Independence: Advanced

General Explanation: Two introductory hours are used to explain the project and determine the order of presentations. Openings require about ten to twenty minutes of class time every day, usually the first thing in the morning, or at the beginning of a class period. Each day one student is responsible for presenting a topic of his or her choice to the rest of the class; in other words, the student teaches for a few minutes. The presentation must have three basic things:

A written report (length can vary)
An oral presentation
A visual display

Goals:

1. To bring current events, history, science, or other subjects into the classroom for daily discussion.
2. To promote the concept of "kids teaching kids."
3. To require the use of research skills as students learn about specific topics.
4. To place emphasis on independent learning.

During This Project Students Will:

1. Select topics to study.
2. Practice using research skills independently as they study and prepare to teach about a topic without teacher assistance.
3. Synthesize ideas from their research into a written report.
4. Design and produce visual aids to use during their oral presentations.
5. Formulate answers to questions asked by classmates about topics.

Skills:

Preparing bibliographies	Sentences
Collecting data	Handwriting
Library skills	Persistence
Making notecards	Controlling behavior

Summarizing
Writing
Organizing
Outlining
Selecting topics
Following and changing plans
Following project outlines
Meeting deadlines
Paragraphs
Accepting responsibility
Concentration
Individualized study habits
Grammar

Time management
Personal motivation
Sense of "quality"
Creating presentation strategies
Drawing and sketching
Poster making
Public speaking
Self-confidence
Teaching others
Neatness
Spelling
Divergent-convergent-evaluative thinking

Handouts Provided:

- "Student Assignment Sheet"
- "Student Evaluation Sheet"
- Teacher's Introduction to the Student Research Guide (see Appendix)
  a. "Poster Evaluation"
- Student Research Guide (see Appendix)
  a. "Things to Check Before Giving Your Presentation"
  b. "Visual Aids for the Oral Presentation"
  c. "Things to Remember When Presenting Your Project"

PROJECT CALENDAR:

HOUR 1: _____	HOUR 2: _____	HOUR 3: _____
Introduction to the project. Students are given an assignment sheet and an evaluation sheet is posted for their review. Distribute handouts from the Student Research Guide. HANDOUTS PROVIDED PREPARATION REQUIRED	Order of presentations is determined (one student per day) and potential topics are discussed.	Two weeks following Hour 2, the first opening is presented. One opening per day is given from this time on, requiring 15 minutes per opening. STUDENTS TURN IN WORK
HOUR 4: _____	HOUR 5: _____	HOUR 6: _____
HOUR 7: _____	HOUR 8: _____	HOUR 9: _____

Lesson Plans and Notes

HOUR 1: Introduce students to "openings" and explain the requirements of the project. A list of topics can be supplied, or students can be allowed to choose their own. Clearly define the subject area (current events, history, famous people, inventions, and so forth) and outline the limits of choice (no movie stars, sports heroes, or "Mickey Mouse" topics). Hand out assignment sheets and material from the Student Research Guide, and post an evaluation sheet for students to study. Discuss various kinds of visual displays; it is helpful to have examples of posters, dioramas, and murals to show. Tell students to think of one or two possible topics for the next hour.

HOUR 2: Decide the order of presentations during this hour. Tell students that openings will begin in two weeks and that the first five or six presenters will be graded less strictly than the rest of the class. These first few presenters will have to face critical analysis as the class discusses how their openings could have been improved and the teacher points out flaws in presentation skills. This is of immense value to later presenters, and early presenters are graded accordingly. Positive reinforcement should also be given along with a word about this being a learning process. The first opening a student does will naturally have room for improvement and this is to be expected. After this is explained, give students slips of paper and tell them to write their names on the slips. There will be two drawings to determine the order of presentations. The first drawing is volunteers only; people who either like to go first or who want less strict grading. After this, the remaining students put their names in the hat and the drawing is completed. Post this list of names in the room. Each student must record a topic next to his or her name at least one week before the presentation is given. Openings begin two weeks from the day of the drawing and continue one per day until everyone in the class has done one. Then a new subject area can be selected and a new round of openings assigned.

The remainder of Hour 2 (after the order of presentations is determined) is spent discussing topics that students may be interested in studying.

General Notes About This Project:

- "Openings" can be a valuable tool for introducing and evaluating presentation skills. Since only one opening is presented each day, you can expect them to improve gradually as students hear your criticisms, praises, and comments to individual presenters.

- Written reports that are required for openings should be turned in and carefully graded for basic writing and language skills.

- Posters should be displayed for at least a week after they are turned in. Students study them to get ideas for their own visual displays, and they add interest to the classroom.

- After each opening a few minutes should be provided for the class to ask questions of the presenter, discuss the strong points, or offer *constructive* criticism of the presentation.

- After questions are answered by the presenter, students often have further questions about the topic. This is a perfect opportunity for you to expound on the subject, explain related ideas, or hold a class discussion if time permits.

- You may decide to use the evaluation sheet that is provided with this project, or you may want to use one or more of the detailed evaluation sheets that are included in the Teacher's Introduction to the Student Research Guide. Be sure to explain your grading system to students before they give their openings.

- Openings offer an excellent opportunity to require students to use the checklists that are supplied in the Student Research Guide.

- Higher-level thinking skills can be emphasized by focusing on key verbs that describe what a student did to produce an opening. Emphasize these verbs as you discuss a student's presentation:

organize	analyze	create	justify
apply	compare	hypothesize	solve
construct	contrast	predict	prove
draw/sketch	categorize	infer	dispute
put in order	separate	compose	judge

OPENINGS
Student Assignment Sheet

An "opening" is a presentation that you will make in front of the class about a topic of your choice. Only one student will present each day and all the students will know well in advance when theirs are due. You will choose your topic from a general emphasis area that is assigned by your teacher. Examples of such areas are:

Current events   Inventions and inventors

Environmental study   Plants

History   Pioneer Life

Science   Futures

Animals   Personal choice

Famous people

A research project that you do at home is truly an independent undertaking. You will collect information, organize it, and teach others about what you have learned. Working at home to produce a project for school is valuable because you will use skills that are necessary for *any* independent project. As you work on your opening, think about how these skills might apply to other activities in your life and things you would like to do in the future. If you see that they are important, then it makes sense to work at improving your ability to use them. Here are eight skills that you will be using: Reading, Writing, Research, Planning, Problem Solving, Self-discipline, Self-evaluation, Presentation. By using these skills properly you will prove to yourself, your friends, and your teacher that you can learn on your own. This makes "Openings" an interesting and challenging project.

The Assignment:

The general emphasis area for this project will be: _____
To prepare for an opening, choose a topic and begin studying it as soon as possible. Watch the news, read newspapers and magazines, write letters, ask questions, read books—inform yourself! For an opening you are required to:

1. Give an oral report to the class. This must be well presented and informative.

2. Design a visual display that shows something about the topic you are presenting. This display is usually a poster, but you may want to make a diorama, mural, scrapbook, model or use an overhead projector, chalkboard, filmstrip, or handout.

3. Prepare a written report and hand it in. This report may be used during your presentation. It should be correctly written and will be graded for basic English and writing skills. If the class does another round of openings later in the year, you may be required to make your presentation from notecards instead of a written report. These notecards will then be handed in and graded.

4. Answer questions from the class at the end of your opening. You should understand your topic well enough to answer most *reasonable* questions. If you don't know the answer to a question, admit it! *Don't make up answers!* You are not expected to be the world's foremost expert, but you *are* expected to spend time to become informed about your topic.

An evaluation sheet for openings will be posted in the room for you to examine. It lists all of the areas on which you will be graded, and how much each is worth. Your opening is worth a total of 100 points.

Name _____ Date _____

OPENINGS
Student Evaluation Sheet

I. Presentation (36 points possible)

    A. Eye contact   2 pts. _____

    B. Voice projection   2 pts. _____

    C. Use of the English language   2 pts. _____

    D. Inflection   2 pts. _____

    E. Accurate information   8 pts. _____

    F. Information is easy to understand 6 pts. _____

    G. Enough information   6 pts. _____

    H. Effort   8 pts. _____

                                        Subtotal _____

II. Visual or extra materials (36 points possible)

    A. Information is easy to understand 4 pts. _____

    B. Neatness   4 pts. _____

    C. Art skills   4 pts. _____

    D. Information is relevent to the oral report 4 pts. _____

    E. Information is current   4 pts. _____

    F. Information is accurate   4 pts. _____

    G. Enough information   4 pts. _____

    H. Effort   8 pts. _____

                                        Subtotal _____

III. Written report (16 points possible)

    A. Report is neatly and correctly written 6 pts. _____

    B. Information is clear and easily understood 4 pts. _____

    C. Information is accurate   6 pts. _____

                                        Subtotal _____

IV. Question-Answer period (12 points possible)

    A. You should be able to answer most reasonable questions about
       your topic   12 pts. _____

              (100 points possible) TOTAL _____

Parent's Signature _____

(Required for scores of 60 or lower)

KIDS TEACHING KIDS

Teacher Preview

Length of Project: 17 hours
Level of Independence: Advanced
Goals:

1. To require the use of research skills as students learn about specific topics.
2. To gain insight into learning by teaching.
3. To place emphasis on independent learning.

During This Project Students Will:

1. Use the independent study skills they have mastered to choose and research topics.
2. Write simple lesson plans and tests.
3. Teach their mini-lessons to a class.

Skills:

Preparing bibliographies	Controlling behavior
Collecting data	Taking care of materials
Library skills	Time management
Making notecards	Personal motivation
Summarizing	Sense of "quality"
Concentration	Creating presentation strategies
Writing	Poster making
Persistence	Drawing and sketching
Organizing	Public speaking
Outlining	Self-confidence
Setting objectives	Teaching others
Selecting topics	Neatness
Following project outlines	Spelling
Meeting deadlines	Divergent-convergent-evaluative thinking
Accepting responsibility	
Individualized study habits	Following and changing plans

Handwriting   Paragraphs
Grammar   Sentences

Handouts Provided:

- "Student Assignment Sheet"
- Student Research Guide (optional) (see Appendix)

PROJECT CALENDAR:

HOUR 1: _____	HOUR 2: _____	HOUR 3: _____
Introduction to the project; students get assignment sheets.	Library research: students decide what their topics will be.	Library research: students receive approval of their topic selections and work on bibliographies. Books are checked out so they can be used in the classroom.
HANDOUT PROVIDED	STUDENTS TURN IN WORK	RETURN STUDENT WORK STUDENTS TURN IN WORK
HOUR 4: _____	HOUR 5: _____	HOUR 6: _____
Bibliographies are handed back and research is conducted in the classroom from books that were borrowed from the library.	Students conduct research and finish notecards.	Notecards are returned to students. Ways of organizing lesson plans are discussed before students begin planning lessons and teaching materials of their own.
RETURN STUDENT WORK	STUDENTS TURN IN WORK	RETURN STUDENT WORK
HOUR 7: _____	HOUR 8: _____	HOUR 9: _____
Work on lesson plans and teaching materials.	Finish work on lesson plans and teaching materials.	Students receive their lesson plans back and are shown how to create tests from them. Then students begin writing tests for their own projects.
	STUDENTS TURN IN WORK	RETURN STUDENT WORK

PROJECT CALENDAR:

HOUR 10: _____	HOUR 11: _____	HOUR 12: _____
Finish writing tests.	Students receive their tests back. These, and the presentations which begin next hour, are discussed.	Student presentations.
STUDENTS TURN IN WORK	RETURN STUDENT WORK	

HOUR 13: _____	HOUR 14: _____	HOUR 15: _____
Student presentations.	Student presentations.	Student presentations.

HOUR 16: _____	HOUR 17: _____	HOUR 18: _____
Student presentations.	Student presentations and wrap-up discussion.	

Lesson Plans and Notes

HOUR 1: Introduce students to the project with a discussion about teaching and how kids can teach other kids. Ask the students: "What kinds of things do you teach each other?" The discussion takes its own course, but obvious examples like the rules of games, slang, skills such as jumping rope or riding a bicycle, homework problems, and behavior patterns should be mentioned. Then tell students that they have the potential to teach things to other students in an educational setting, and that "Kids Teachings Kids" is designed to help them choose a topic, find information, develop lesson plans, make a test, and actually teach a mini-class (ten to fifteen minutes). Hand out assignment sheets and spend the remainder of the hour discussing the project requirements.

Notes:

- To be less time consuming, Hours 12 through 17 can be redesigned as a small-group activity. The first eleven hours remain the same, but the presentation time is reduced.

- If students are very advanced independent learners, this project can be a homework assignment. In this case, Hour 1 should provide due dates for material to be handed in and for final presentations. The assignment sheet should be carefully explained.

- If any of the checklists from the Student Research Guide are to be used during the project, they should be handed out during this hour.

- The assignment sheet states that students will design a way to teach something to younger students. They should be informed during this hour if they are really going to get an opportunity to teach younger children or if their lesson will be presented to their classmates.

HOUR 2: Students go to the library for general research. Each student chooses a topic to study and turns it in on a notecard at the end of the hour.

Notes:

- Be sure to evaluate the topic choices students make. Don't let anyone pursue a topic that has insufficient information or that is frivolous in nature. The topic should be specific enough to cover in one lesson. Require students who choose broad, general topics to narrow them down.

- The research activity is done primarily in general references and is designed to help students choose interesting topics. Encourage them to spend the entire hour, with an open mind, browsing through books before definitely deciding upon a topic.

HOUR 3: Students go to the library to conduct research on the topics they have chosen. At the beginning of the hour return their topic choices to them with either an "approval" or "disapproval." Students who do not have approved topics meet with you or a librarian to choose new topics. This hour is spent working on bibliographies. Students turn in references to at least three sources at the end of the hour.

Note:

- If it is not convenient for you to go to the library, you should have students check out the books they need so that classes can be held in the classroom from this point on. If using the library is no problem, continue meeting there.

HOUR 4: Return bibliographies and tell students to begin working on notecards.

HOUR 5: Students work on notecards and hand them in at the end of the hour.

Note:

- An evaluation sheet for notecards is provided in the Teacher's Introduction to the Student Research Guide.

HOUR 6: Hand back the notecards and devote the first half of the hour to a discussion of lesson plans and how they are written. Encourage students to produce very simple plans. They are to make a complete list of the facts they want to teach and develop a plan for teaching those facts. The plan can be an outline that shows the order in which facts will be presented along with the method of presentation (lecture, chalkboard, overhead, poster, discussion, question-answer, handout, and so forth). The remainder of the hour is spent working on lesson plans and teaching materials.

HOUR 7: Work on lesson plans and teaching materials continues.

HOUR 8: Lesson plans and teaching materials are finished by the end of the hour. If more time is needed by some students, the work is done at home. Lesson plans are handed in.

Note:

- The most important consideration when evaluating your students' lesson plans is that they be *simple*. If a plan seems complicated, it will probably be difficult or impossible for the student who developed it to teach.

HOUR 9: Lesson plans are returned and the first half of the hour is devoted to a discussion about writing test questions. Emphasize simplicity. Encourage students to write multiple-choice questions with four possible answers, making certain that one answer is definitely correct. Examples of good test items should be presented to give an idea of how to phrase questions. Tell students that writing a test is not easy and that they must be very careful about accuracy and adherence to the information presented during the lesson. The remainder of the hour is spent working on tests.

HOUR 10: Tests are finished by the end of the hour. Students hand their tests in to be checked.

HOUR 11: Return the tests. The hour is spent in discussion about the tests and the kinds of things that need to be rewritten. Most students will have some work to do on their tests. The remainder of the hour is a general discussion about the presentations that will begin next hour.

HOURS 12, 13, 14, 15, and 16: Students make their presentations.

Notes:

- After each presentation, a few minutes should be provided for questions from the class.

- Evaluation sheets for oral reports and posters are provided in the Teacher's Introduction to the Student Research Guide.

- If it is possible, make arrangements for students to present their lessons to another class, preferably to students one or two years younger than they are.

HOUR 17: If time is needed for more presentations, it is taken from this hour. The hour is designed to offer a discussion of higher level thinking skills and how they were used during this project. In Benjamin S. Bloom's *Taxonomy of Educational Objectives** there are six categories, beginning with the lowest level, knowledge, and progressing through comprehension, application, and analysis to the two highest levels, synthesis and evaluation. This project requires students to work at all six levels, but emphasis during the project is placed on *synthesis:* the ability to draw together ideas or components from diverse sources to create something new. This is exactly what students did to develop their lesson plans; in fact, teaching is an excellent example of synthesis. Center the discussion on action verbs that describe what students *did* that allowed them to teach a class: create, imagine, combine, suppose, predict, add to, role play, hypothesize, design, invent, infer, improve, synthesize, adapt, compose, change, *teach.*

---

*Benjamin S. Bloom, editor, *Taxonomy of Educational Objectives, Book One: Cognitive Domain* (New York, NY: Longman, Inc., 1954, 1956), p. 18.

Name _____ Date _____

KIDS TEACHING KIDS
Student Assignment Sheet

One of the most exciting things about independent learning is that you can become an "expert" about a subject that your friends may not understand. "Kids Teaching Kids" allows you to share your knowledge with others. The process of teaching requires you to do much more than acquire knowledge, however, and that is what this project is all about. You will be *synthesizing* information, which means that you will take facts that are known and build them into something that has not existed before. You are going to create something new!

For this project you will select a topic that is of interest to you and then design a way to teach something about it to younger kids. Be sure to select a topic that you can work with; don't choose something that is too difficult to understand or explain. The simpler the topic is, the easier it will be to teach to kids one or two years younger than you. Do the following to complete this project:

I. Choose a subject that is educational (for example, Indians, airplanes, World War II, art, electricity, weather, insects, volcanoes, trains, famous people, the space program, or health food). The topic you choose from this subject area must be approved by your teacher before you begin research. Make this topic specific enough to explain or describe in one lesson.

II. Research your topic.

    A. Find at least three good sources of information that are *not* encyclopedias and make a bibliography card for each. In addition, you may use as many encyclopedias as you wish.

    B. Find at least twenty facts about your topic and record them on notecards.

III. Design a lesson plan.

    A. Think of a way to teach kids one or two years younger than yourself about the facts you have learned from your research. Such things as a handout, lecture, game, story, poster, puppet show, demonstration, information written on a chalkboard, or anything else you can think of should be used to make your lesson interesting.

    B. Write down your lesson plan and hand it in to be checked. Include the following:

        1. A list of things you want the class to learn. Be as specific as possible.
    Example: My students will learn these things about space satellites:

          a) Four satellites that have made history:

            (1) Sputnik
            (2) Explorer
            (3) Telstar
            (4) Space lab

          b) How many satellites are presently orbiting the earth.
        c) Ten uses for man-made satellites.
        d) How data are transmitted and received from satellites.
        e) How satellites are put into orbit.

        2. A list of materials you will need to teach the lesson.
      3. A written description of how you plan to organize the lesson. You may do this in outline form, but be thorough and carefully record everything you intend to do.
    Example:

          a) Display a poster that shows various satellites, their purposes, and the dates they were launched.
        b) Present a brief time line of satellite history.
        c) Give examples of specific satellites and how they are used.
        d) Describe how satellites are put into orbit.
        e) Explain how one particular satellite works, in detail, with models and drawings.
        f) Discuss possible future uses for satellites.
        g) Answer questions from the class.

IV. Write a test.

    A. Make up a ten-question test to give the class when your lesson is finished.
  B. The questions should be multiple choice. Be sure they are written simply and clearly.
  C. Each question must relate directly to something presented in the lesson.

V. Teach your lesson.

    A. You will teach your lesson *after* graded materials are returned. (You may be required to rewrite some of your materials if they are written poorly.) Remember that your lesson is designed to teach kids who are one or two years younger than you are. If you don't get a chance to actually work with this type of audience, then your classmates will have to role play a group of younger students while you give the lesson.
  B. Your presentation will be evaluated for accuracy of information and the quality of your bibliography, notecards, lesson plan, and test.

VI. Use this chart to record project due dates:

    A. Bibliography cards   Due_____
  B. Notecards   Due_____
  C. Lesson plan   Due_____
  D. Presentation   Due_____

THAT WAS THE YEAR

Teacher Preview

Length of Project: 21 hours
Level of Independence: Advanced
Goals:

1. To promote in-depth study of history or historical periods.
2. To place emphasis on small-group interaction and cooperation.
3. To require the use of research skills as students learn about specific historical events.
4. To promote the concept of "kids teaching kids."
5. To place emphasis on independent learning within a group.

During This Project Students Will:

1. Follow an outline to complete project requirements.
2. Learn on their own in small groups.
3. Conduct research and collect facts about their group's topics.
4. Prepare proper bibliographies and notecards.
5. Produce a mural/collage.
6. Explain murals in group presentations to the class.
7. Evaluate their own work and the work of others in the group.

Skills:

Preparing bibliographies	Accepting responsibilities
Collecting data	Concentration
Observing	Controlling behavior
Library skills	Following project outlines
Listening	Individualized study habits
Making notecards	Persistence
Summarizing	Sharing space
Grammar	Taking care of materials
Handwriting	Time management
Neatness	Personal motivation
Paragraphs	Self-awareness

Sentences
Spelling
Group planning
Organizing
Setting objectives
Selecting topics
Divergent-convergent-evaluative
  thinking
Following and changing plans
Identifying problems
Meeting deadlines
Writing

Sense of "quality"
Setting personal goals
Creative expression
Creating presentation strategies
Drawing and sketching
Poster making
Public speaking
Self-confidence
Teaching others
Working with others
Working with limited resources

Handouts Provided:

- "Student Assignment Sheet"
- "Final Evaluation"
- "Student Self-Evaluation"
- Student Research Guide (optional; see Appendix)

PROJECT CALENDAR:

HOUR 1: _____ Introduction to the project. Students receive assignment sheets, followed by a discussion about the kinds of topics a group might choose. HANDOUT PROVIDED PREPARATION REQUIRED	**HOUR 2:** _____ Brief year-by-year synopsis of history (from 1929 to the present) outlined by the teacher. PREPARATION REQUIRED	**HOUR 3:** _____ Discussion about which decade to study. Students vote for one decade at the end of the hour.
HOUR 4: _____ Students vote for the year they want to study. Small groups of four to five students are identified.	**HOUR 5:** _____ Each group lists the topics from the assignment sheet in order of preference. A draft is conducted to choose topics.	**HOUR 6:** _____ Students conduct research.
HOUR 7: _____ Research continues.	**HOUR 8:** _____ Research continues.	**HOUR 9:** _____ Research continues.

PROJECT CALENDAR (continued):

HOUR 10: _____	HOUR 11: _____	HOUR 12: _____
Last day of research.	Notecards are turned in at the beginning of the hour. Each person's mural topic is determined and groups begin planning their murals.	Notecards are returned and groups continue planning their murals.
	STUDENTS TURN IN WORK	RETURN STUDENT WORK
HOUR 13: _____	HOUR 14: _____	HOUR 15: _____
Students begin working on their murals.	Work on murals.	Work on murals.
NEED SPECIAL MATERIALS	NEED SPECIAL MATERIALS	NEED SPECIAL MATERIALS
HOUR 16: _____	HOUR 17: _____	HOUR 18: _____
Work on murals.	Work on murals.	Students must finish murals by the end of the hour.
NEED SPECIAL MATERIALS	NEED SPECIAL MATERIALS	NEED SPECIAL MATERIALS

PROJECT CALENDAR (continued):

HOUR 19:	HOUR 20:	HOUR 21:
Develop and practice mural presentations.	Students present their murals to the class. Self-evaluation sheets are handed out at the end of the hour.	Discussion about the murals and group dynamics. Self-evaluation forms are turned in.
	HANDOUT PROVIDED	STUDENTS TURN IN WORK
HOUR 22:	HOUR 23:	HOUR 24:
HOUR 25:	HOUR 26:	HOUR 27:

Lesson Plans and Notes

HOUR 1: Give students their assignment handouts and introduce the project. Discuss the importance of the ability to work together. Tell the class that they will be divided into small groups of four to five students later in the project (Hour 4), and that each group will have an assignment to complete. The specific assignment will be determined by the students themselves. The first task for "That Was the Year" is to select a decade and then a year to study. This part is done as a class. Spend the hour discussing the range of choice (any year from 1929 to the present) and the kinds of information a small group might be able to find about a particular year.

   Notes:

   • It is important to explain the grading or evaluation system that will be used before the project gets under way, so students understand what they are being evaluated for. Talk to them about the self-evaluation form, too.

   • Prepare for the first two hours by compiling a varied list of major historical events that have occurred since 1929. This need not be a massive research project, but it is important to be comfortable enough with history to take a two-hour walk down memory (or history) lane with your students. These first two hours of the project prepare the class to choose a year to study. If you feel inadequate in relating history to your students, consider bringing in a guest speaker to lay the groundwork for this project.

   • It is not easy to find information about a *year;* what do you look up if you want to find out what happened in 1950? Students will need help understanding the process of looking up topics and then confining themselves to information that pertains to the year they are studying. The process may require three steps: use time lines or general histories to find the year that is being studied; examine that portion of the time line for clues to topics that can be looked up; look up those topics and isolate the events or facts that are most appropriate for the project. Also, past *Readers' Guides to Periodical Literature* can be used to pinpoint periods in time and identify topics.

HOUR 2: A brief year-by-year synopsis of history, from 1929 to the present, is given. Even though this will touch only on the largest events, it will help students decide which era they would like to study. The Great Depression, World War II, the first man on the moon, President John F. Kennedy's assassination, the bicentennial, the Olympics, Martin Luther King's speech, entitled "I Have a Dream," opening the door to China, the Vietnam War, the "Cold War," and the advent of the computer are just a few of the historical happenings that can be discussed. At the end of this hour tell students to think about what *decade* they would most like to study, and to come to the next hour prepared to explain their choices.

Notes:

- Films, filmstrips, guest speakers, readings, television shows, or other support materials can be incorporated into the first two or three hours of this project to help introduce students to historical events. The introduction can be expanded by one or two hours if you have a number of such materials to present.

- A writing assignment can be helpful at this point, to help determine on which decade the class will focus. Ask each student to select a decade and write a one-page paper defending the selection: why would it be a good decade to study? These papers should be done as homework and read in class during Hour 3.

HOUR 3: Students come to class prepared to discuss the decade on which they would like to concentrate; each student is allowed to give an opinion, and the hour is spent discussing the decades that various students have nominated. After the discussion, students vote on which decade to concentrate. Run-off votes should be conducted until one decade has over 50 percent of the vote. The decision about which *year* the class is finally going to choose will be made at the beginning of the fourth hour. Encourage students to talk with their parents, relatives, and friends about which year might be most interesting.

Note:

- Students should be encouraged to look through encyclopedias at home or at a local library to discover and record some interesting events from the decade that has been chosen. Tell them to record the *year* the event occurred. This exercise will help Hour 4 go smoothly, when students vote for a year to focus on during the project.

HOUR 4: Students nominate the year they prefer to study and give reasons for deciding upon that year. If more than one year is nominated, hold an election. If there are no nominations, hold a drawing. Divide the class into small groups of four or five students. Decide in advance how groups will be chosen. If time remains, have students meet in their small groups.

Note:

- You may want to reduce the size of small groups to three students if there is enough space and materials to allow such a reduction. Three students will have easier access to the mural than five; it is difficult to have five students all working on a mural at the same time unless it is very large. If the primary reason for using this project is group interaction and decision making, however, use the larger group size to ensure a diversity of opinion.

HOUR 5: Each group studies a different set of topics for "That Was the Year." To decide what these will be, a selection process called a "topic draft" is conducted. This is like the draft professional football teams go through each year when they select top college prospects. Before the topic draft, each group creates a list showing its preference of topics taken from the assignment sheet. All forty-three topics should be included in this priority list. During the draft each group claims one topic at a time as the opportunity to choose goes from group to group. When a group has as many topics as it has members, it is ready to begin the project. Each group member must find facts and information about *all* the topics his or her group has drafted, or chosen.

Note:

- When students select their group's topics, it is important to emphasize that no topic "belongs" to a specific person. If there are four students in a group, the group will choose four topics and each student will collect information on all four. After the research is completed, a drawing is held to determine which topic each student will be responsible for on the mural. This helps ensure that everyone will work hard at selecting acceptable topics and finding adequate information, because information is shared by everyone in the group.

HOUR 6: Students study group topics in almanacs, encyclopedias, history books, magazines, newspapers, and other reference sources. It is very important that they have access to a library.

HOURS 7, 8, and 9: Students continue doing research.

HOUR 10: Students continue their research. They are told that they will turn in their notecards and bibliographies at the beginning of the next hour.

HOUR 11: Students turn in notecards and bibliographies. The rest of the hour is spent determining which topic each student will be responsible for on his or her group's mural. This decision should be made by drawing and not by vote, since it is not fair to let aggressive or "pushy" students get what they want, leaving what remains to others. If time is still available, students begin planning their murals.

Note:

- Notecards and bibliographies are collected to ensure that every person has done an adequate job of collecting information and neatly recording it; the intention is not to grade each card strictly. You can tell at a glance if a set of notecards has been carefully produced. Sloppy, incomplete, or inaccurate work should be done over. If a student refuses to cooperate or to put quality and effort into his work, it may be necessary to give him or her a separate research project that will not interfere with the group's efforts. Do this only as a last resort, but be sensitive to the other group members and their desire to do a good job.

HOUR 12: Return notecards and bibliographies to their owners. Students trade cards with other members so that each person has *all* of the group's notecards on one particular topic. Students continue planning their murals until each member of the group knows what his or her part of the final mural will look like. The rest of the hour, if time remains, is spent studying notecards and discussing the information and how it should be presented on the mural.

HOUR 13: Students begin work on their murals.

Notes:

- The materials for producing a mural should be on hand at the beginning of this hour. These materials will be needed for the next five hours. A basic list of materials includes mural paper, markers, pencils, erasers, rulers, meter sticks, glue or paste, colored construction paper, compasses, and ink pens.

- The mural/collages ideally should be made on large sheets of rolled paper or some other large-format paper that can be written on with pencil and ink. If available table space does not allow four or five students to sit around one piece of paper, it may be necessary to have each group member produce a poster or collage at his or her own desk and combine these later into one display.

HOURS 14, 15, 16, and 17: Students work on murals.

HOUR 18: Students finish their murals by the end of the hour. Inform groups that they will present their work to the class during Hour 20 and that they will have Hour 19 to prepare for this.

HOUR 19: Students develop and practice their mural presentations.

HOUR 20: Students present their murals to the class. At the end of the hour the murals are put on display. Give students self-evaluation forms to fill out at home and turn in during Hour 21.

Note:

- Additional evaluation sheets for oral reports, posters (or murals), and notecards are provided in the Teacher's Introduction to the Student Research Guide.

HOUR 21: After collecting self-evaluation forms, hold a wrap-up discussion, focusing first on the quality of the murals and the variety of ideas that emerged from this project. Then turn the discussion to group dynamics and personal interactions that occur in a project like this. Ask students to discuss or give examples of what they learned from the way their group:

Chose topics	Shared information
Brainstormed ideas	Settled disagreements
Made decisions	Helped each other
Compromised opinions	Presented finished murals
Planned murals	Evaluated each other

General Notes About This Project:

- A great deal can be done to narrow the focus of this project. For example, reduce the time-span from which students can choose to a single decade that is determined before they are introduced to the project. Or, predetermine an area of emphasis, such as science or politics or famous people, and require that all groups choose their topics from this area. In other words, begin "That Was the Year" with the stipulation that the class will study science in the 1950s or politics in the 1960s. Students must then generate lists of specific topics for individual research.

- Student progress should be carefully monitored to ensure that it coincides with the hour-by-hour description that is provided. Depending on the students, the environment, and the accessibility of reference material, this project may require more or less time than is allowed for here. After you have conducted the project once, it will become obvious how many hours each activity will require for your particular situation.

- Topics may be added to the list in the student handout; the more the better.

- Encourage students to share ideas and information with each other. Everyone in the class is studying the same year; students in one group are bound to run across material that someone in another group can use. The project can be looked upon as a full-class activity in which *everyone* is working together to learn as much as possible about one particular year. From this perspective, sharing facts and materials is an integral part of the final product.

- This is not an easy research project; it is designed for students who already have the necessary skills for finding information and developing projects independently. Guidance and supervision are essential; be actively involved in the project, especially as a problem solver. Get others involved if you can, such as the librarian, a student teacher, parents, volunteers, or school aides. The twin goals of independent learning and interpersonal cooperation rely heavily upon organization, resource availability, assignment clarity, specific student responsibilities, and most important, student confidence that they are capable of the task. If you provide proper training, a structured but relaxed classroom atmosphere, and encouraging assistance throughout the project, valuable lessons about individual and group learning will be gained by everyone involved.

- There are many ways to modify, restructure, or supplement this project. Here are two ideas:

—A class file for all of the bibliography cards can be established so that everyone has access to the sources that have been discovered.

—Groups can be assigned specific *months* of the year to study, instead of topics, and produce a combined time line. This works best with recent years because more information is available.

Name _____ Date _____

THAT WAS THE YEAR
Student Assignment Sheet

This is a small-group project. Each group member's contribution is important and will affect the final outcome of the project. Part of your assignment is to plan with others, help make decisions, complete your share of the work, and accept other people's points of view. The ability to work with others, even if you don't get your way all of the time, is a skill that will help you in many ways throughout life.

It is important to understand at the outset of "That Was the Year" that you are being taught how to find information on your own *and* how to combine what you know with the ideas and knowledge of others. Learning on your own does not always mean working by yourself. Life is full of situations where people must work together to accomplish their goals. Families, committees, governing bodies, scout groups, sports teams, and a company's employees are all examples of groups where people work together.

Pay attention to the kinds of problems that occur during this project and the way different people react to working in small groups. Keep in mind that everyone has something to contribute, though some may be better at communicating it than others.

Here is the rest of your assignment:

I. As a class, choose a *decade,* or a ten-year period, that you would like to study. After talking in class about some of the major historical events that have happened since 1929 (this may require two or more class hours), you will vote on which of these decades you would like to look at more closely:

1930–1939   1970–1979
1940–1949   1980–1989
1950–1959   1990–beyond
1960–1969

Come to class on the day of the vote prepared to nominate one of the decades as your choice. Be ready to give three or four good reasons to explain why you would prefer to study that ten-year period. You may be required to record your reasons in writing and turn them in.

II. After a decade has been chosen, think about which year from that decade you would like the class to concentrate on. A year will be selected by a vote or by a drawing; if enough students in the class want one specific year, a vote will establish that year for the project. If there is much disagreement, a drawing will be held.

III. You will be placed in a small group (three to five students) by your teacher. Complaining and expressing disapproval of these groups should be held to a minimum; your job is to work as well as you can with your partners, regardless of who they are.

THAT WAS THE YEAR (continued)

IV. Your group will meet and write the topics from this handout in order of preference on a separate sheet of paper. Number one will be the topic your group *most* wants to study and number forty-three will be the *least* desirable topic. In class there will be a "topic draft" (a drawing will determine the order in which groups will select topics). One at a time, each group will draft a topic from the list. After the first round each group will have one topic, and then the second round will begin. There will be as many rounds as there are people in your group, so if you have four people in your group, you will choose four topics in the draft. Each topic can be studied by *one* group only. If another group drafts a topic that you have high on your list, you will cross it off and go to your next choice.

TOPICS

automobiles	politicians
fashions	Supreme Court decisions
movies	cost of living
movie stars	great achievements
radio and television	women's movement
farming	civil rights
sports	famous or infamous people
technology	the economy
inventions	international trade
medicine	communism in the world
legislation	population (national and world)
the president	industry
war	airplanes
natural disasters	space age
fads	photography
foreign leaders	dance
weather	architecture
unions and labor movement	trains
gangsters and terrorists	political issues
music	great events
art	the president's cabinet
scientific discoveries	

V. You are responsible for studying *all* of your group's topics, recording facts on notecards, and providing a bibliography. The number of people in your group determines how many facts you will find for each topic.

If your group has:	*you must find:*
2 people (2 topics)	20 facts about each topic
3 people (3 topics)	13 facts about each topic
4 people (4 topics)	10 facts about each topic
5 people (5 topics)	8 facts about each topic
6 people (6 topics)	7 facts about each topic

VI. You will be given five hours of classroom or library time to conduct research and record facts. You may locate additional information on your own time if you want.

VII. On a date set by your teacher, you will turn in all of your notecards and a bibliography. These will be checked to see if you fulfilled the requirements of the project and for neatness, organization, and quality.

VIII. After your notecards are turned in, your group will have a drawing to see which topic each person will be responsible for on the mural. Write each of your group's topics on a separate slip of paper and put the slips in a hat or box. Draw one slip per person; the topic you draw is the topic you will represent on your mural.

IX. When you get your graded notecards back, you will trade with other members in your group; for example, if the topic you drew is "airplanes," you will collect all of the notecards about airplanes from your fellow group-members to combine with your own airplane cards. At the same time you will give your other cards to the people who drew those topics. Now you have all of your group's information about airplanes and you are ready to begin working on your section of the mural. Remember that your fellow group-members' bibliographies are valuable resources for you. They will tell you where to go to get further details about the topic; be sure to use them!

X. Your group will discuss what it wants its mural/collage to look like: its arrangement, lettering, each person's section, how to connect each section, and any other considerations you can think of.

XI. Once you have determined where your section of the mural/collage will be and how it is to be arranged, you may begin work on it. You will be given six class-hours to complete it. Here are the *minimum* requirements for your part of the mural/collage:

A. Present *at least* twenty of the facts that the group has collected about your topic. You may present these facts in any way you wish: drawings, diagrams, charts, pictures, sentences, or any other method that others can understand.

B. Include *at least* two of your own original drawings to show something about your topic. It is effort and not artistic ability that is important here.

XII. When your mural/collage is completed, your entire group will present its work to the class. You will be given one class-hour to develop and practice this demonstration. When your group's presentation is done, its mural/collage will be put on display and the project will be completed.

THAT WAS THE YEAR
Student Self-Evaluation

List the people in your group (including yourself) below. As fairly and as honestly as you can, give each person an evaluation for the four categories to the right of the names. Circle a number under each category: "1" is poor, and "5" is excellent.

NAME	COOPERATION	EFFORT	QUALITY	NEATNESS/ ORGANIZATION
1. _____ _____	1 2 3 4 5	1 2 3 4 5	1 2 3 4 5	1 2 3 4 5
2. _____ _____	1 2 3 4 5	1 2 3 4 5	1 2 3 4 5	1 2 3 4 5
3. _____ _____	1 2 3 4 5	1 2 3 4 5	1 2 3 4 5	1 2 3 4 5
4. _____ _____	1 2 3 4 5	1 2 3 4 5	1 2 3 4 5	1 2 3 4 5
5. _____ _____	1 2 3 4 5	1 2 3 4 5	1 2 3 4 5	1 2 3 4 5
6. _____ _____	1 2 3 4 5	1 2 3 4 5	1 2 3 4 5	1 2 3 4 5

Name _____ Date _____

THAT WAS THE YEAR
Final Evaluation

I. Topic Research

    A. Bibliography   5 pts. _____

    B. Notecards

        1. Accuracy   5 pts. _____

        2. Neatness   5 pts. _____

        3. Written in your own words   5 pts. _____

                                            Subtotal _____

II. Mural/Collage

    A. Working with others   10 pts. _____

    B. Contribution to the finished mural   10 pts. _____

    C. Effort   10 pts. _____

    D. Neatness   5 pts. _____

    E. Taking care of materials   5 pts. _____

                                            Subtotal _____

III. Final Presentation

    A. Eye contact, use of hands, posture   5 pts. _____

    B. Voice projection, articulation, inflection   5 pts. _____

    C. Effort   5 pts. _____

    D. Accuracy   5 pts. _____

                                            Subtotal _____

IV. Student Self-Evaluation (average scores from group members)

    A. Cooperation   5 pts. _____

    B. Effort   5 pts. _____

    C. Quality   5 pts. _____

    D. Organization/neatness   5 pts. _____

                                            Subtotal _____

                                TOTAL.......100 pts. _____

Teacher's Comments: _____

_____

R-10

INDEAPENDENT PROJECT

Teacher Preview

Length of Project: 4 hours
Level of Independence: Advanced
General Explanation: Even though this is an independent project on which students work at home, three hours of class time are needed for them to get organized and have project proposals approved. An additional hour is needed at the end of the project for students to present finished work. Since Hours 2 and 3 aren't "full" classroom hours, you may want to add a discussion about specific project ideas to each.

Goals:

1. To allow students to design and produce an independent project.
2. To require the use of research skills as students learn about specific topics.

During This Project Students Will:

1. Select topics to study.
2. Design their own projects.
3. Apply the research skills they have learned.
4. Work independently to complete the requirements of their project contracts.

Skills:

Preparing bibliographies	Accepting responsibility
Collecting data	Individualized study habits
Library skills	Persistence
Making notecards	Time management
Summarizing	Personal motivation
Controlling behavior	Taking care of materials
Setting objectives	Concentration
Writing	Sense of quality
Neatness	Creating presentation strategies
Spelling	Drawing and sketching
Organizing	Poster making
Outlining	Public speaking

85

Selecting topics

Following and changing plans

Following project outlines

Meeting deadlines

Grammar

Handwriting

Self-confidence

Teaching others

Divergent-convergent-evaluative thinking

Paragraphs

Sentences

Handouts Provided:

- "Student Contract/Requirements Sheet"
- Student Research Guide (optional; see Appendix)

PROJECT CALENDAR:

HOUR 1:	HOUR 2:	HOUR 3:
Introduction to the project. Students are given their contract/requirements sheets. A discussion of topic possibilities follows.	Project proposals are collected. Projects are not started until proposals are returned to the students with signed contracts during Hour 3.	Project proposals are returned. Those that are adequately completed are accompanied by a signed contract. Students work on their projects at home until they are due (Hour 4).
HANDOUT PROVIDED	STUDENTS TURN IN WORK	RETURN STUDENT WORK
HOUR 4:	HOUR 5:	HOUR 6:
Finished projects are turned in or presented.		
STUDENTS TURN IN WORK		
HOUR 7:	HOUR 8:	HOUR 9:

Lesson Plans and Notes

HOUR 1: Introduce students to the project and hand out contract/requirements sheets. Place emphasis on *independence;* this project will be done at home on the students' own time. Students are allowed to choose their topics (within reason!), but they must *plan* their projects, write proposals, and receive signed contracts before they can begin. Give a due date when project proposals are to be turned in for approval.

HOUR 2: Collect proposals with attached contracts. Tell students to wait until their proposals are approved before beginning their projects, as changes may be required.

HOUR 3: Return project proposals. Those proposals that were properly produced are accompanied by a contract with your signature. These contracts are to be signed by the students and returned to you to be kept on file. Students who do not receive a signed contract meet with you for an explanation of what can be done to make their proposals acceptable.

HOUR 4: Finished projects are turned in (or presented). The time line for this due date is variable and depends on the abilities of the students, course schedules, and other demands on students' time.

General Notes About This Project:

- This project is not designed to teach a certain set of skills; its sole purpose is to let students display their ability to design their own learning experiences.

- You may decide to grade or evaluate any or all of the things that have been emphasized in the preceding projects in this book. However, it is important to be aware of "self-evaluation" as a necessary part of independent learning. This might be a convenient time to grade simply on completion, and let students take credit for whatever is produced. In other words, these projects should stand or fall on their own merit; let students decide for themselves if their work is "good enough." They will know better than anyone else.

- One copy of the signed contract should be given to the student and one should be kept on file. It is a good idea to photocopy the proposal as well, so that a complete record of the project is available if it is needed.

- Students should be required to keep daily logs of their work during this project. They record progress, problems encountered, and new ideas they think of. For students who run into difficulty completing their projects, the daily log can provide a basis for you to help them get back on track. A "Daily Log" is provided in the Student Research Guide.

Name _____ Date _____

INDEPENDENT PROJECT
Student Contract/Requirements Sheet

TOPIC _____

Independent study means working on your own to learn about something. It takes a skilled learner to choose a topic, find information, organize and record facts, plan a project, and present a finished product to other people. Successfully completing an independent project indicates that a person has the ability to think for him- or herself. Discovering that you have this ability is an important step in building self-confidence and represents a milestone in your educational experience.

This contract allows you to design your individualized project. You might want to do a project on astronomers, lasers, butterflies, the stock market, or one of many other possible topics. Create your own area of study by following the five steps below to prepare for the project. These five requirements are to be turned in for approval; a signed contract from your teacher means your proposal has been approved and that you may begin working on your topic.

I. Describe the things you will do to complete your project. For example: write a report and build a model; or, make a poster, write a report, and give a demonstration in front of the class. Choose at least two different ways of showing what you have learned with your project and describe them in detail.

II. Make an outline that shows each step of your project; in other words, write a description of how the project will progress from one stage to the next, step by step. This is a project plan and you will be expected to follow it. It will help determine what to do first, second, third, and so on until the project is completed.

III. Make drawings of any models, dioramas, murals, posters, or other visual displays you plan to build or make. These drawings should show how things will fit together and how space is going to be used.

IV. Write a short explanation of where information for your project will come from, and include a bibliography. Will you use the library? Will you write letters, make phone calls, interview people, or use articles from magazines? Explain where and how you will find material for your subject. Locate some key sources of information *before* you begin the project, to be sure it is possible to do what has been proposed.

V. Make a list of materials that will be needed to complete the project. This list should include *everything,* even pencils and paper.

After these five requirements are completed, turn your project proposal in to be checked. Once this contract is signed by your teacher, the project is approved and work can begin. An independent project is something to take seriously, so give it your best effort and produce something to be proud of.

_____ has completed all assignments, is passing all courses, has completed the five steps required to design an independent project, and is hereby allowed to work on a project entitled _____.

Date _____ Student's signature _____

Teacher's signature _____

APPENDIX

Teacher's Introduction to the Student Research Guide

Many of the projects in *Learning on Your Own!* require students to conduct research. Few children, however, possess the necessary skills to complete this type of project successfully. The Research Guide is designed to help them learn and practice some basic skills: how to locate, record, organize, and present information about topics they study. Even though the handouts in the guide are detailed, students will need some guidance and instructional support from you as they undertake their first research projects.

This teacher's introduction to the guide contains three forms that can be used to evaluate how well students do on (1) notecards, (2) posters, and (3) oral presentations. These are designed as optional evaluations that may be used with many projects in the book, regardless of subject or topic area.

Teaching a lesson on "how to use the library" is one type of instructional support you should give students to prepare them for research. A "Typical Library Quiz" is also included in this teacher's introduction for you to give students after they have become acquainted with the library.

The Student Research Guide will be most useful to students if you spend some time explaining the following topics to your class:

1. *Library skills:* Use an example of a real library to explain how books and periodicals are categorized and where they are stored. Whatever library is most likely to be used by students should serve as a model. Cover these things in a library skills unit:

   a. The card catalog (handout provided)
   b. How to find a book from its call number (handout provided)
   c. The *Readers' Guide to Periodical Literature* and other periodical guides (handout provided)
   d. How to ask questions and use librarians as helpful resources
   e. Other kinds of information and services offered by libraries

2. *Notecards and bibliographies:* Provide a variety of examples of properly made notecards and bibliographies for students to use as models. (Reference handout provided.) Explain how to use a numbering system to cross-reference a set of notecards with a bibliography. Spend enough time on bibliographies to ensure

that students know how to write them for the most common sources (books, magazines, encyclopedias, and newspapers).

3. *The Readers' Guide to Periodical Literature:* You can teach students how to use this valuable resource before they ever go to a library. Contact the librarian and ask for old monthly *RGPL* discards. Collect them until you have at least one for every student in the room. During your library skills unit pass the guides out and write ten topics on the board, for example:

    a. The president of the United States
    b. The automobile industry
    c. Basketball (or football, baseball, hockey, and so forth)
    d. Ballet
    e. Acid rain
    f. Poland
    g. Israel
    h. Martin Luther King, Jr.
    i. Satellites
    j. Agriculture

    Tell students to choose five topics; find at least one article about each; and properly record the title of the article, the author of the article, the name of the magazine, its volume number, the pages on which it can be found, and the date it was published.

4. *Common sources of information:* Encourage students to make extensive use of encyclopedias, magazines such as *National Geographic, Junior Scholastic, Newsweek,* and others that are readily available, textbooks and workbooks, materials from home, and whatever other sources are in the classroom or school library. Always require that adequate information from these common sources be available before allowing a research project to begin.

The Student Research Guide is primarily a series of handouts. You may want to give them to students as a complete booklet or hand them out individually to be used with separate, specific research lessons. The Research Guide is supplied as an aid to help students tackle projects that require research and independent work. The handouts *supplement* what is being taught in projects and provide excellent reference materials for independent learning.

Name _____ Date _____

NOTECARD EVALUATION

Below are ten areas for which your notecards have been evaluated. This breakdown of your final score, which is at the bottom of the sheet, indicates the areas where improvement is needed and where you have done well.

	EXCELLENT (10 pts.)	VERY GOOD (9 pts.)	GOOD (7 pts.)	FAIR (6 pts.)	POOR (4 pts.)	NOT DONE OR INCOMPLETE (0 pts.)
1. Bibliography	____	____	____	____	____	____
2. Reference between notecards and bibliography	____	____	____	____	____	____
3. Headings and subheadings	____	____	____	____	____	____
4. Organizing information onto cards so it can be understood and used later without confusion: numbering system	____	____	____	____	____	____
5. Neatness (If reading or use of the cards is made difficult because of sloppy writing, "POOR" will be checked.)	____	____	____	____	____	____
6. Recording meaningful information (Everything recorded on notecards should relate directly to your topic.)	____	____	____	____	____	____
7. Spelling	____	____	____	____	____	____
8. Accuracy of information	____	____	____	____	____	____
9. Quantity (Did you do as much work as you were supposed to, or should have, to complete the project?)	____	____	____	____	____	____
10. Information properly recorded (Facts must be brief and understandable. It is best to condense information into concise statements. Entire paragraphs should not be copied onto notecards. Direct quotes must be identified.)	____	____	____	____	____	____

FINAL SCORE _____ (100 possible)

COMMENTS _____

_____

_____

Name _____ Date _____

POSTER EVALUATION

Below are ten areas for which your poster has been evaluated. This breakdown of your final score, which is at the bottom of the sheet, indicates the areas where improvement is needed and where you have done well.

	EXCELLENT (10 pts.)	VERY GOOD (9 pts.)	GOOD (7 pts.)	FAIR (6 pts.)	POOR (4 pts.)	NOT DONE OR INCOMPLETE (0 pts.)
1. Facts which your poster teaches (at least twenty)	_____	_____	_____	_____	_____	_____
2. Poster "goes along with" your written report	_____	_____	_____	_____	_____	_____
3. Visual impact: use of color, headings, and lettering	_____	_____	_____	_____	_____	_____
4. Drawings (at least one)	_____	_____	_____	_____	_____	_____
5. Pictures, articles, headlines, quotes, charts, graphs, diagrams, explanations, and so forth	_____	_____	_____	_____	_____	_____
6. Organization of material	_____	_____	_____	_____	_____	_____
7. Neatness	_____	_____	_____	_____	_____	_____
8. Spelling, grammar, writing skills	_____	_____	_____	_____	_____	_____
9. Accurate information	_____	_____	_____	_____	_____	_____
10. Specific topic; proper material (Did you do a good job of presenting your topic?)	_____	_____	_____	_____	_____	_____

FINAL SCORE _____ (100 possible)

COMMENTS _____

_____

_____

Name _____ Date _____

ORAL PRESENTATION EVALUATION

This form shows how your oral presentation has been evaluated. It indicates areas where improvement is needed and where you have done well.

Topic _____

I. Presentation (50 points possible)

    A. Eye contact.   3 pts. _____
    B. Voice projection.   3 pts. _____
    C. Use of the English language.   3 pts. _____
    D. Inflection.   3 pts. _____
    E. Articulation.   3 pts. _____
    F. Posture.   3 pts. _____
    G. Use of hands.   3 pts. _____
    H. Appropriate vocabulary.   3 pts. _____
    I. Accurate information.   10 pts. _____
    J. Information is easy to understand.   3 pts. _____
    K. Enough information.   3 pts. _____
    L. Information relates to topic.   3 pts. _____
    M. Effort.   7 pts. _____

    Subtotal _____

II. Visual or Extra Materials (30 points possible)

    A. Information is easy to understand.   3 pts. _____
    B. Information relates to the oral report.   3 pts. _____
    C. Information is current.   3 pts. _____
    D. Information is accurate.   3 pts. _____
    E. Enough information.   3 pts. _____
    F. Neatness.   3 pts. _____
    G. Spelling.   3 pts. _____
    H. Artistic effort.   3 pts. _____
    I. Research effort.   3 pts. _____
    J. Appropriate vocabulary.   3 pts. _____

III. Question-Answer Period (20 points possible)

    A. Confidence in knowledge of topic.   3 pts. _____
    B. Ability to answer reasonable questions.   3 pts. _____
    C. Answers are accurate.   3 pts. _____
    D. Student is willing to admit limits of knowledge or understanding such as "I don't know."   2 pts. _____
    E. Answers are brief.   3 pts. _____
    F. Student exhibits ability to infer or hypothesize an answer from available information.   3 pts. _____
    G. Student appears to have put effort into learning about this topic.   3 pts. _____

    Subtotal _____

    TOTAL (100 points possible) _____

COMMENTS _____
_____
_____
_____

© 1987 by The Center for Applied Research in Education, Inc.

Name _____ Date _____

TYPICAL LIBRARY QUIZ

How well do you know the library? Answer these questions and find out.

1. List four kinds of information you can find on a card in the card catalog:

   a. _____

   b. _____

   c. _____

   d. _____

2. What does "jB" tell you about a book when it precedes the call number?

   _____

3. What does "jR" tell you about a book when it precedes the call number?

   _____

4. Suppose you are writing a report about polar bears. You look up "polar bears" in the card catalog but find only a few sources. What would you look under next?

   _____

5. If you are looking for a book with the call number j598.132/D43, would you find it before or after j598.2/D42?

   _____

6. If you are looking for "G-men" in the card catalog, you may find a card that says "G-men, see U.S. Federal Bureau of Investigation." Where would you look next?

   _____

7. List these call numbers in the order that they would be found on the shelf:

   j973.15   j973.35   j973.3   j973
   Ad32   Ab24   Cy31   Ad55

   a. _____   c. _____

   b. _____   d. _____

8. Books of fiction are shelved alphabetically by _____.

9. Biographies are shelved alphabetically by _____.

10. What do the words or letters on the front of a card catalog drawer tell you? (example: Istanbul—jets)

   _____

11. For how long can books be checked out of the library?

   _____

12. If the book you are looking for is not on the shelf, what should you do?

   _____

13. Where would you go to find a listing of all the magazines your library subscribes to? (Circle the correct answer.)
   a. Card catalog
   b. History and travel
   c. Information desk
   d. Young adults
   e. *Readers' Guide to Periodical Literature*

14. For *current* information, where should you check first?
   a. Encyclopedia
   b. *Readers' Guide to Periodical Literature*
   c. Card catalog
   d. Book shelves
   e. Reference shelves

15. Below is an excerpt from the *Readers' Guide to Periodical Literature*. Look it over and then answer the questions:

   The real cost of a car. S. Porter, il Ladies Home J. 99:58 Je '82

   a. What is the title of the article? _____
   b. Who wrote the article? _____
   c. What month and year was the article published? _____
   d. What magazine published the article? _____
   e. In what volume of the magazine was the article published? _____
   f. On what page can the article be found? _____
   g. Where in the library would you be most likely to find this article?

   _____

Student Research Guide

STUDENT RESEARCH GUIDE

Research is the process you go through to find information about a topic that interests you. This guide explains some basic tools needed to find and record information. It gives advice about how to conduct a research project and also provides many suggestions for developing a *presentation* of the topic.

A list of skills that you will use during research projects includes finding resources, choosing topics, writing and note taking, summarizing, organizing ideas, scanning, planning, and interpreting data. This guide will help in many of these areas.

Of course, the real quality of a project is determined by the personal characteristics you bring to it—things like patience, motivation, accuracy, neatness, humor, persistence, and creativity. There are no handouts in the Student Research Guide that teach these things, but they are perhaps the most essential ingredients of a successful project.

Your Research Guide contains the following handouts:

"Outlining"
"Bibliographies"
"Notecards and Bibliographies"
"Sending for Information"
"The Dewey Decimal Classification System"
"The Card Catalog"
"*The Readers' Guide to Periodical Literature*"
"Choosing a Subject"
"Audio-Visual and Written Information
    Guides"

"Where to Go or Write for Information"
"Project Fact Sheet"
"Sample Project Fact Sheet"
"Poster Display Sheet"
"Things to Check Before Giving Your
    Presentation"
"Visual Aids for the Oral Presentation"
"Things to Remember When Presenting Your
    Project"
"Daily Log"
"Blank Skills Chart"

Name _____ Date _____

OUTLINING

I. Outlining is like classification: it sorts ideas and facts into categories or like-groups. This is an important skill to have when you are conducting a research project because you must organize information before you can use it.

II. Outlining separates main ideas from details in two ways:

A. By symbols   I.
   1. Alternating letters and numbers   II.
   2. Same symbol = same importance   A.
B. By indentation   B.
   1. Indent more with each subheading   1.
   2. Same margin = same importance   2.
                  a)
                  b)
                    (1)
                    (2)

OUTLINING (continued)

III. It is very important to understand that every item in an outline can be expanded with additional research or new information. The outline below is incomplete, but it shows how to use symbols and indentation to organize facts and ideas into a logical order. When you make an outline, leave plenty of room between lines so additional ideas can be included later. Think of ways to expand this outline:

EXAMPLE: My Autobiography

I. Early years

  A. Birth

    1. Place

    2. Date

    3. Time

    4. Other details

  B. Family

    1. Father

    2. Mother

    3. Brothers and sisters

    4. Other members of the extended family

    5. Other important adults in your life

  C. First home

    1. Location and description

      a) address

      b) type of house

      c) color

      d) trees in yard

        (1) tall maple in back

        (2) two cherries in front

        (3) giant oak in side yard

          (a) rope swing

          (b) tree house

          (c) shade

            i. summer afternoon naps

            ii. lemonade stand three summers ago

    2. Neighborhood

    3. Experiences

II. School years

  A. School or schools attended

    1. School name and description

    2. Favorite teacher(s)

    3. Favorite subject(s)

  B. Significant experiences

    1. Vacations

    2. Births

    3. Deaths

    4. Adventures

    5. Ideas and beliefs

  C. Friends

III. Present

  A. Residence

  B. Family

  C. School

  D. Hobbies and interests

  E. Friends

IV. Future

  A. Education

  B. Career

  C. Personal goals

  D. Vacations—trips

  E. Family

BIBLIOGRAPHIES

A bibliography is a standard method for recording where information came from. It is important to be able to prove that research came from legitimate sources. Use the following forms when recording information for bibliographies:

I. When working with a book:

    A. Author's last name first
    B. Full title underlined
    C. Place of publication
    D. Date of publication
    E. Publisher
    F. Page(s)

NOTECARD FORM:

Galbraith, John K.
The Affluent Society
Boston
1966
Houghton Mifflin
76

STANDARD FORM:

    Galbraith, John K., The Affluent Society. Boston: Houghton Mifflin, 1966; 76.

II. When working with a periodical:

    A. Author's last name first
    B. Full article title in quotes
    C. Name of periodical underlined
    D. Volume number
    E. Date in parentheses
    F. Page(s)

NOTECARD FORM:

Lippmann, Walter
"Cuba and the Nuclear Race"
Atlantic
211
(Feb. 1963)
55-58

STANDARD FORM:

    Lippmann, Walter. "Cuba and the Nuclear Race." Atlantic 211 (February 1963): 55-58.

III. When working with newspaper articles:

    A. Author's last name first
    B. Full article title in quotes

    C. Name of paper underlined
    D. Date
    E. Section (some papers are not divided into sections)
    F. Page

NOTECARD FORM:

May, Clifford D.
"Campus Report: Computers In, Typewriters Out"
The New York Times
May 12, 1986

28

STANDARD FORM:

    May, Clifford D. "Campus Report: Computers In, Typewriters Out," The New York Times, May 12, 1986, p. 28.

IV. When working with an encyclopedia:

    A. Author's last name first
    B. Full title of article in quotes
    C. Name of encyclopedia underlined
    D. Date of publication in parentheses
    E. Volume number
    F. Page(s)

NOTECARD FORM:

Clutz, Donald G.
"Television"
Encyclopaedia Britannica
(1963)
21
910

STANDARD FORM:

    Clutz, Donald G. "Television," Encyclopaedia Britannica (1963), 21, 910.

NOTECARDS AND BIBLIOGRAPHIES

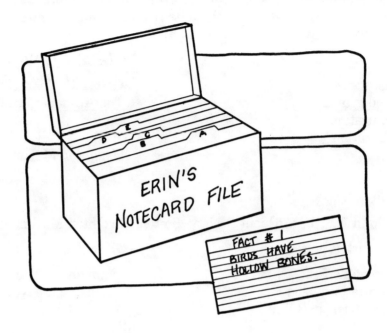

Notecards are used to record and collect information. Bibliography cards are used to tell where the information came from. Once information is gathered about a topic, notecards become the main tool for writing a report. Since each notecard contains a separate idea, you can arrange and rearrange these ideas into an order that becomes an outline for your report. If more information is needed about a particular fact, or, if something needs to be clarified, bibliography cards will tell which source to go to.

Each card should be numbered. It is *very* important that each notecard have a bibliography card number to tell where each fact came from. For example, if you study a unit called "Ecology" in science class, you could do a project about air pollution. Suppose you found information about air pollution in a book titled *Environmental Pollution*—you would make one bibliography card for this source, regardless of how many facts you obtained from it. If this book was the fifth source you used, the bibliography card for it would be numbered "5" in the upper right.

Now, suppose that the chapter on air pollution has four facts, or pieces of information, that you want to use. Make four notecards, each with a unit or course title at the top ("Ecology") and the topic being studied on the next line ("air pollution"). Number these cards in the upper right-hand corner, continuing the numbers from the last card of your fourth source. In other words, if you have 17 notecards from your first four sources, the next card you make will be number 18.

Next, tell where you found the information on each notecard. Do this by writing "bibliography card #5" at the bottom right of each of these four notecards. This clearly shows that you have to look at bibliography card number five to find out where the information came from.

Remember to put only one important fact on each notecard. Don't copy long passages from sources onto notecards; condense information into easily stated facts. If a quote is included in your report, however, it *should* be recorded word for word. Also, if you record your bibliography on notebook paper instead of notecards, each source must still be numbered.

Here is a sample notecard:

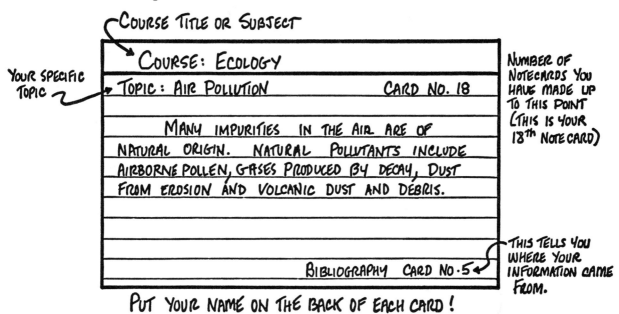

COURSE TITLE OR SUBJECT

YOUR SPECIFIC TOPIC

COURSE: ECOLOGY

TOPIC: AIR POLLUTION   CARD NO. 18

MANY IMPURITIES IN THE AIR ARE OF NATURAL ORIGIN. NATURAL POLLUTANTS INCLUDE AIRBORNE POLLEN, GASES PRODUCED BY DECAY, DUST FROM EROSION AND VOLCANIC DUST AND DEBRIS.

BIBLIOGRAPHY CARD NO. 5

NUMBER OF NOTECARDS YOU HAVE MADE UP TO THIS POINT (THIS IS YOUR 18th NOTE CARD)

THIS TELLS YOU WHERE YOUR INFORMATION CAME FROM.

PUT YOUR NAME ON THE BACK OF EACH CARD!

If you are required to record your bibliography on notecards, here is a sample bibliography card:

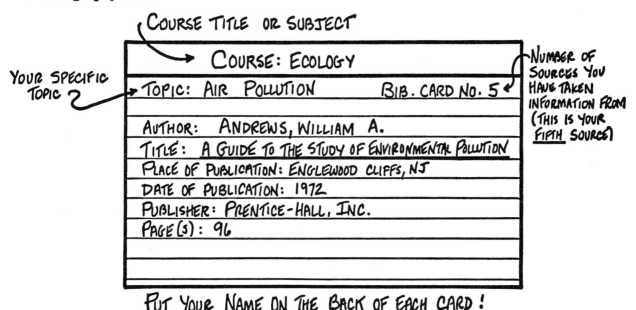

COURSE TITLE OR SUBJECT

YOUR SPECIFIC TOPIC

COURSE: ECOLOGY

TOPIC: AIR POLLUTION   BIB. CARD NO. 5

AUTHOR: ANDREWS, WILLIAM A.
TITLE: A GUIDE TO THE STUDY OF ENVIRONMENTAL POLLUTION
PLACE OF PUBLICATION: ENGLEWOOD CLIFFS, NJ
DATE OF PUBLICATION: 1972
PUBLISHER: PRENTICE-HALL, INC.
PAGE(S): 96

NUMBER OF SOURCES YOU HAVE TAKEN INFORMATION FROM (THIS IS YOUR FIFTH SOURCE)

PUT YOUR NAME ON THE BACK OF EACH CARD!

SENDING FOR INFORMATION

There are times when sending a letter is the best way to obtain information about a research topic. Unfortunately, many people write letters hastily. They don't take time to explain themselves clearly or else they come across sounding unprofessional and insincere. You should learn how to write a good letter so that, when confronted with a difficult project, you can get help from others. Study the outline below. It explains why letter writing is a useful research skill and what components should be included in the letters you write. Examples of two letter styles are provided.

I. Reasons for sending a letter:
   A. To obtain up-to-date information.
   B. To make contact with experts or specific organizations.
   C. To get specialized or technical information.
   D. To ask for opinions and advice.
   E. To ask for suggestions of other places to look for information about the topic.
   F. To ask for free materials.
   G. To send special questions to authorities in the field you are studying.

II. Parts of a letter

A. Heading:	*Your* return address at the top of the letter, and the date right below your address.
B. Inside address:	The address of the person or organization to whom you are sending the letter.
C. Salutation:	Begin your letter with a salutation to the person you are sending it to: Dear Mr. Wilson; Dear Miss Goode; Dear Mrs. Smith; Dear Ms. Jones; Dear Sir.
D. Body:	Introduce yourself, explain your project, and ask for whatever assistance you are seeking. Be concise and clear in your writing; don't make someone guess what you want.
E. Complimentary close:	Show your respect by thanking the person to whom you have sent your letter for whatever help he or she can provide. Your letter might end like this:

"...I appreciate any advice or information you can offer to help me with my project.
Thank you."

                                                          Sincerely,

                                                          John Jones

F. Signature	Sign your name at the bottom of the letter, beneath the complimentary close.

Example of the "Block Letter" Style

John Jones
1532 Hill Street
Bridgeton, TX 75588

March 16, 19XX

Dr. David Adamson
Entomological Society
113 Geneva Road
Fair Ridge, OH 45289

Dear Dr. Adamson:

I am an eighth-grade student at Bridgeton Middle School, and we are doing a science project on insects. I am studying the praying mantis, and I have three questions that I can't find answers to from my research. I thought maybe you could help me.

I have enclosed a self-addressed, stamped envelope for your convenience. Here are my questions:

1. By what other names are praying mantises known?
2. How many species are there?
3. Can young praying mantises fly?

I appreciate any information you can provide about these questions. Thank you.

Sincerely,

John Jones

John Jones

Example of a "Modified Block Letter" Style

Dr. David Adamson
Entomological Society
113 Geneva Road
Fair Ridge, OH 45289

March 22, 19XX

John Jones
1532 Hill Street
Bridgeton, TX 75588

Dear John,

I received your letter of March 16, and I am glad to help you. Here are my answers to your questions:

1. The praying mantis is also known by these names: rearhorse, mule killer, devil's horse, and soothsayer.

2. There are 20 species of praying mantis. The European mantis is well established in the eastern U.S., and the Chinese mantis has also established itself in the eastern states.

3. One female lays up to 1,000 eggs in the fall, which hatch in May or June. The young cannot fly; they grow slowly, acquiring wings and maturity in August. When mature, four well-developed wings allow slow, extended flight.

I hope this information helps you in your research work. By the way, thank you for enclosing a stamped envelope—I appreciate that. If I can be of further assistance, please let me know.

Sincerely,

David Adamson, M.D.

Dr. David Adamson

DEWEY DECIMAL CLASSIFICATION SYSTEM

1. The Dewey Decimal Classification System arranges all knowledge into ten "classes" numbered 0 through 9. Libraries use this system to assign a "call number" to every book in the building. A call number is simply an identification number that tells where a book is located in the library.

   (000) 0—Generalities
   (100) 1—Philosophy and related disciplines
   (200) 2—Religion
   (300) 3—The social sciences
   (400) 4—Language
   (500) 5—Pure sciences
   (600) 6—Technology (applied sciences)
   (700) 7—The arts
   (800) 8—Literature and rhetoric
   (900) 9—General geography, history,
           and so forth

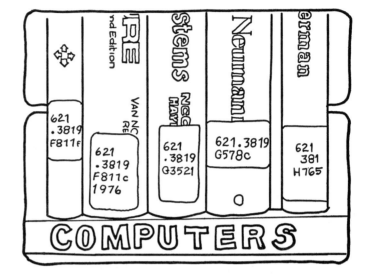

2. Each *class*, with the use of a three-digit number, is divided into ten subclasses (divisions) with the first division (600–609) set aside for the general works on the entire class. For example, 600–649:

   600–609 is given over to *general works* on the applied sciences
   610–619 to the medical sciences
   620–629 to engineering and applied operations
   630–639 to agriculture and agricultural industries
   640–649 to domestic arts and sciences

3. Each division is separated into ten subclasses or "*sections*" with the first "*section*" (630) devoted to the general works on the entire *division*. For example:

   630 is assigned to agriculture and agricultural industries in general
   631 to farming activities
   632 to plant diseases and pests and their control
   633 to production of field crops
   636 to livestock and domestic animals, etc.

4. Further subdividing is made by following the three-digit number with a decimal point and as many more digits as is necessary. For example, 631 farming is divided into

   631.2 for farm structures
   631.3 for farm tools, machinery, appliances
   631.5 for crop production

5. In summary, every book in a library is assigned a call number based upon the Dewey Decimal Classification System. All library books are stored on shelves according to their numbers, making them easy to find.

6. To locate a book in the library follow these steps:

   a. Use the card catalog to find the call number of a book in which you are interested. Books are cataloged by author, title, and subject.
   b. Record the call number, usually recorded in the upper left-hand corner of the card. If your library uses a computerized catalog system, ask a librarian for assistance in locating the call number.
   c. Refer to the first three numbers of the call number to determine in which section of the library your book can be found.
   d. Once you have found this section of the library, use the rest of the call number to locate the book on the shelf.

Name _____ Date _____

THE CARD CATALOG

The card catalog is usually the first place you would go to look for a book in the library. The cards in the card catalog are arranged alphabetically by subject, author, and title. The card below is a "subject" card, filed under "inventors." The same book could be found if you looked under "Manchester, Harland Frank" (along with any other books Mr. Manchester has written) or *Trailblazers of Technology* (the title of the book).

Once you find the card that best fits your needs, the most important piece of information is the "call number" in the upper left-hand corner. This number tells you where to find the book in the library. In trying to decide which book to look up, you may refer to various pieces of information found on every catalog card. This information includes

1. Call number
2. Subject
3. Author
4. Author's birth date
5. Title
6. Brief description
7. Illustrator (if there is only one)

8. Location of publisher (city)
9. Publisher
10. Date of publication
11. Number of pages
12. Whether or not the book is illustrated
13. Size of the book

Here is a sample card:

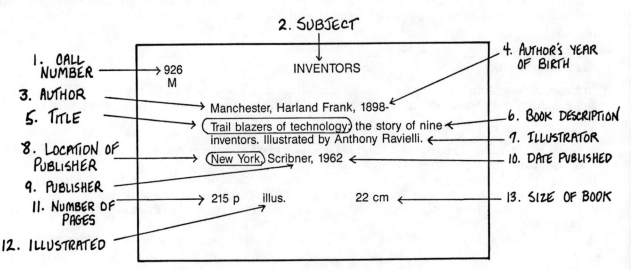

READERS' GUIDE TO PERIODICAL LITERATURE

The *Readers' Guide to Periodical Literature* is an extremely useful tool. You can find magazine articles about current topics from as recent as one or two months ago. You can also find articles that were written fifteen, twenty, or fifty years ago. Subject and author headings are arranged alphabetically in the *Guide*. Articles are arranged alphabetically under each heading.

When a promising reference is found, first determine how to locate the magazine that published the article. Does the library subscribe to the magazine? Is it a current issue? (Usually issues for the past twelve months will be available in the periodical reading section of the library.) Are old issues recorded on microfilm, or are they bound and placed in a special area of the library? When you find an article you want to read, record the following on a piece of paper. Then you or a librarian, if necessary, can locate the magazine from its file area.

The elements in each entry are:

1. Title of the article
2. Author's name
3. Name of the magazine
4. Volume number
5. Pages on which the article can be found
6. Date of publication

Suppose you are studying atomic power; specifically, you want to find out about the costs of building and operating atomic power plants. By looking through a *Readers' Guide*, you will find many articles published about atomic power. From the example provided you can see that "atomic bombs" is at the top of the list of atomic topics, followed by atomic energy, atomic energy industry, atomic facilities, atomic fuels, atomic power, atomic power industry, atomic power plants, and atomic research. There, under "Atomic power plants—Economic aspects," is a collection of five articles that could be useful to you. Look at the fourth one:

Whoops! A $2 billion blunder. C.P. Alexander. il *Time* 122:50-2 Ag 8 '83
1. Title: "Whoops! A $2 Billion Blunder"
2. Author: C.P. Alexander
3. il: this article is illustrated with photographs or drawings
4. Magazine: *Time*
5. Volume: 122
6. Page(s): 50-52
7. Date: August 8, 1983

READERS' GUIDE TO PERIODICAL LITERATURE (continued)

The *Readers' Guide to Periodical Literature* makes use of abbreviations for months of the year, magazine names, and other pieces of important information. For example, "Bet Hom & Gard" is *Better Homes and Gardens* and "bi-m" means a magazine is published bimonthly. Be sure to refer to the first few pages of the *Readers' Guide* for a complete list of all the abbreviations used.

The following is a section from the *Readers' Guide to Periodical Literature:*

Atomic bombs
                            History
    See also
  Hiroshima (Japan)
                  Physiological effects
    See Radiation—Physiological effects
                        Testing
    See Atomic weapons—Testing
Atomic energy *See* Atomic power
Atomic energy industry *See* Atomic power industry
Atomic facilities *See* Nuclear facilities
Atomic fuels *See* Nuclear fuels
Atomic power
    See also
  Anti-nuclear movement
  Nuclear fuels
                  Economic aspects
    See also
  Atomic power industry
                Laws and regulations
    See also
  Radioactive waste disposal—Laws and regulations
  Mixed rulings on nuclear power [Supreme Court decisions] R. Sandler. *Environment* 25:2-3 Jl/Ag '83
                Germany (West)
    See also
  Anti-nuclear movement—Germany (West)
Atomic power industry
    See also
  Computers—Atomic power industry use
  Reactor fuel reprocessing
  Washington Public Power Supply System
                Export-import trade
  Firing spotlights plutonium exports [R. Hesketh's claim that plutonium produced in Great Britain's civilian reactors has been used in U.S. weapons manufacture] D. Dickson. *Science* 221:245 Jl 15 '83
                Laws and regulations
    See Atomic power—Laws and regulations
                Public relations
  Atom and Eve [nuclear acceptance campaign geared to women] L. Nelson. il *Progressive* 47:32-4 Jl '83
                United States
    See Atomic power industry
Atomic power plants
                Economic aspects
  The bankruptcy of public power [Washington Public Power Supply System debacle] *Natl Rev* 35:982-3 Ag 19 '83
  Money meltdown [Washington Public Power Supply System default] S. Ridley. *New Repub* 189:11-13 Ag 29 '83
  When billions in bonds go bust [default of Washington Public Power Supply System] *U S News World Rep* 95:7 Ag 8 '83
  Whoops! A $2 billion blunder. C. P. Alexander. il *Time* 122:50-2 Ag 8 '83
  The Whoops bubble bursts. H. Anderson. il *Newsweek* 102:61-2 Ag 8 '83
                Laws and regulations
    See Atomic power—Laws and regulations
             Safety devices and measures
  Computers to supervise nuke plants. *Sci Dig* 91:27 Jl '83
Atomic research
  Pseudo-QCD [discussion of January 1983 article, A look at the future of particle physics] B. G. Levi. *Phys Today* 36:98+ Jl '83

CHOOSING A SUBJECT

The first step in any research project is choosing something to study. This requires some thought and decision making. This handout provides several guidelines that will help you select a subject.

1. Choose a subject that you are already interested in or that you would like to know more about.

2. Choose a subject that will meet the needs or requirements as outlined by the teacher:
   a. Listen for suggestions from the teacher.
   b. Be alert to ideas that come from class discussion.
   c. Talk to friends and parents about things you can study and learn.

3. A good rule by the Roman poet Horace: "Choose a subject, ye who write, suited to your strength." This means pick a subject you can understand, not one in which you will become bogged down, lost, or disinterested.

4. The encyclopedia should serve as a tool for choosing the right subject and narrowing it down so you can handle it:
   a. It gives the general areas of the subject.
   b. It identifies specific topics related to your subject.
   c. It is written simply enough to understand without hours of study.

5. Before you commit yourself to a subject, check to make sure there is some information available. There is nothing more frustrating than starting a project that cannot be finished because there are no books, magazines, filmstrips, newspapers, journals, experts, or even libraries that have enough information.

6. Once you have chosen a subject, write down a series of questions to which you want to find answers. Write as many as you can think of. These questions will help direct your research.

Name _____ Date _____

AUDIO-VISUAL AND WRITTEN INFORMATION GUIDES

DIRECTIONS: The following list shows some of the places where information can be found. When you begin your first project, go down column one and put a check mark in the box next to each place you *might* be able to find information. When you *do* find information, fill in the appropriate box on the chart with your pencil. Do this for your first five research projects.

	PROJECT NUMBER				
	1	2	3	4	5
Almanacs					
Atlases					
Bibliographies					
Biographies					
Charts and graphs					
Dictionaries					
Encyclopedias					
Films					
Filmstrips					
Historical stories					
Indexes to free material					
Letters					
Library card catalog					
Magazines					
Maps					
Microfilm					
Newspapers					
Pictures					
Readers' Guide to Periodical Literature					
Records					
Tapes					
Textbooks					
Vertical files					
Other: _____					

Name _____ Date _____

WHERE TO GO OR WRITE FOR INFORMATION

DIRECTIONS: Before you start your project, put a check mark in the box next to each place you could go or write to get information. When you *do* get information, fill in the appropriate box.

	PROJECT NUMBER				
	1	2	3	4	5
Chambers of Commerce					
Churches					
City officials					
Companies					
Embassies					
Experts					
Factories					
Federal agencies					
Historical societies					
Hobbyists					
Librarians					
Libraries					
Ministers					
Museums					
Newspaper office/employee					
Organizations (club, societies)					
Professionals					
Research laboratories					
State agencies					
Teachers					
Travel agencies					
Universities					
Zoos					
Friends					
Home (books, magazines, etc.)					
Other: _____					
_____					

Name _____ Date _____

PROJECT FACT SHEET

One of the most difficult parts of any project is getting started. Use the "Project Fact Sheet" to begin recording information that will be included in a presentation or report. A sample of a completed "Project Fact Sheet" is shown on the next page.

My topic is _____

and these are the facts I am going to teach the rest of the class:

1. _____

2. _____

3. _____

4. _____

5. _____

6. _____

7. _____

8. _____

9. _____

10. _____

11. _____

12. _____

13. _____

14. _____

15. _____

16. _____

17. _____

18. _____

19. _____

20. _____

Name _____ Date _____

PROJECT FACT SHEET: Example

This completed fact sheet about humpback whales shows how to write out information that is to be included in a presentation.

My topic is <u>Humpback Whales,</u> and these are the facts I am going to teach the rest of the class:

1. Humpback whales spend six months in the South Pacific.
2. Humpback whales sing a strange song that seems to be some sort of communication.
3. Humpback whales sing only when they are in the South Pacific.
4. Humpback whales do not eat when they are in the South Pacific.
5. Humpback whales travel to an Arctic Alaskan bay to feed.
6. A humpback whale has a brain that is five times larger than a human brain.
7. The invention of the explosive harpoon gun and the steam engine made full-scale hunting of the humpback whale possible.
8. Humpback whales show great devotion to one another; this is best displayed by the relationship between a mother and her young.
9. A young whale is called a "calf."
10. The humpback whale eats krill, which makes it a carnivorous mammal.
11. (This list is extended to whatever the project outline requires.)

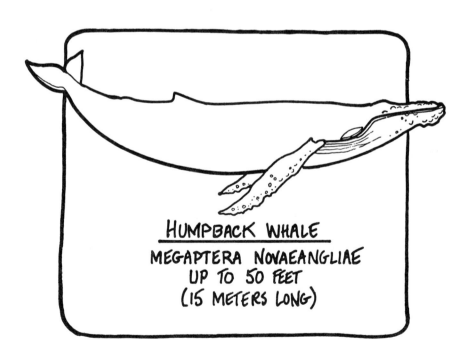

HUMPBACK WHALE
MEGAPTERA NOVAEANGLIAE
UP TO 50 FEET
(15 METERS LONG)

POSTER DISPLAY SHEET

Use the guidelines on this handout if you are required to make a poster for a research project.

1. Present or "teach" at least twenty facts about your topic on the poster. These facts should be recorded on notecards.

2. The poster should be made to go with the written report so that they can be used together when you make a presentation.

3. Include at least one of your own drawings on it.

4. The poster can also have other pictures, magazine articles, newspaper headlines, quotes from books, charts, graphs, illustrations, explanations, diagrams, captions, and so forth.

5. Organize all of the material on the poster so that it is easy to understand. This is very important when making a top-quality poster. Give your poster visual impact by using colorful designs, bold headings, and a catchy title.

6. Writing must be neat! Use parallel guidelines and pencil words in lightly before going over them with marker.

7. Check spelling, grammar, capitalization, punctuation, and sentences to be sure they are correct.

8. Every bit of information you use must be accurate. *Do not make anything up!*

9. Your poster should be about a very specific topic. Don't throw everything you can find onto it. Be selective and use only material that contributes favorably to the project.

10. OPTIONAL: Write five questions that can be answered by studying your poster. These questions should be attached to the poster.

Name _____ Date _____

THINGS TO CHECK BEFORE GIVING YOUR PRESENTATION

DIRECTIONS: After practicing your presentation at home one time, write "yes" or "no" in the boxes below to help determine which areas need more work. The purpose of this checklist is to help put *quality* into your presentation. Use it wisely and be honest. If something needs more time and effort, be willing to admit it and work to improve what you have done.

	PROJECT NUMBER				
	1	2	3	4	5
Have I done enough research?					
Is everything spelled correctly?					
Did I use neat handwriting?					
Is everything in my visual display labeled?					
Do all my pictures have captions?					
Is my visual display neat and attractive?					
Did I use colors in a pleasing way?					
Did I do my best artwork?					
Does my oral report need more practice?					
Do I know all the words in my report?					
Is it easy to understand what I have written?					
Is my report informative?					
Is my visual display informative?					
Do I understand the information I will present?					
Did I choose interesting and different presentation methods?					
Have I decided how I will display my visual materials during my presentation?					
Am I ready to answer questions about my subject?					
Did I follow the project directions or outline?					
Does my presentation stick to my subject?					
Is this my best work?					

Name _____ Date _____

VISUAL AIDS FOR THE ORAL PRESENTATION

DIRECTIONS: Making your report interesting is very important. Besides hearing what you have to say, the audience likes to see examples of what you've done. There are many ways to use visual aids during a presentation. This list provides some suggestions. First, check the items that you think you *could* use. Later, fill in the ones you actually *did* use.

	PROJECT NUMBER				
	1	2	3	4	5
Chalkboard					
Charts					
Clippings					
Diagrams					
Dioramas					
Film (slides)					
Filmstrips					
Guest speakers					
Magazines					
Maps					
Models					
Murals					
Opaque projector					
Overhead projector					
Pictures					
Posters					
Records					
Tape recorder					
Other: _____					
_____					

When speaking to a group you must always be aware of these things:

1. Voice projection
2. Eye contact
3. Inflection

4. Proper grammar
5. Hand control
6. Posture

Name _____ Date _____

THINGS TO REMEMBER
WHEN PRESENTING YOUR PROJECT

Try to remember these rules when you are speaking before the group. Underline the ones you need to improve. On the lines at the bottom of this sheet, write any other rules and notes you feel you need as reminders.

1. Speak in complete sentences.
2. Use any new vocabulary words you may have learned, but be sure you can pronounce them and that you know what they mean.
3. Speak with a clear voice so that everyone can hear.
4. Look at your audience and speak to its members.
5. Stand aside when you are pointing out pictures, maps, charts, drawings, or diagrams.
6. Do not read long passages from your notes.
7. Know your material so that you sound like an informed person.
8. Be as calm as possible. Try to show that you have confidence in your work.
9. Do not chew gum when presenting.
10. Be ready to tell where you got your information.
11. Explain what your visual display shows, but don't read everything that is on it to your audience. Let the audience read it later.
12. Ask for questions from the class.
13. Be willing to admit that you don't know an answer if you really don't know.
14. Never make up an answer. You are expected to give only accurate information.
15. When your project is due to be presented, have it ready in final form—and on time! Do not come to class with empty hands and a list of excuses.

16. _____

_____

17. _____

_____

18. _____

_____

NOTES: _____

_____

_____

HOW TO USE THE DAILY LOG

Directions:

One of the most important requirements of an independent worker is an accurate record of each day's accomplishments. This is especially important for students who are just learning how to do research projects on their own. A Daily Log is helpful because every step of the project is recorded. This allows the teacher to check your progress without watching you work. The more conscientious you are about keeping a detailed, accurate log, the more likely you are to earn the right to become involved in even more independent projects.

To use the log on the next page, simply fill in the date and the time you started working on your project. Describe what you did as accurately as possible and record what was accomplished. Record the time when you are finished.

For example:

Oct. 14   10:45–11:25   Looked in 3 magazines for info. about earthquakes. Recorded facts on 10 notecards. Found 2 poster ideas.

DAILY LOG

Name: _____

Project Title: _____

Date Due: _____ Date Begun: _____ Date Completed: _____

DATE	TIME BEGUN	TIME ENDED	DESCRIPTION OF WORK

SKILLS CHART: RESEARCH

#	**Prerequisite Skills** Students must have command of these skills.
X	**Primary Skills** Students will learn to use these skills; they are necessary to the project.
0	**Secondary Skills** These skills may play an important role in certain cases.
*	**Optional Skills** These skills may be emphasized but are not required.

	RESEARCH									WRITING						PLANNING				
	PREPARING BIBLIOGRAPHIES	COLLECTING DATA	INTERVIEWING	WRITING LETTERS	LIBRARY SKILLS	LISTENING	MAKING NOTECARDS	OBSERVING	SUMMARIZING	GRAMMAR	HANDWRITING	NEATNESS	PARAGRAPHS	SENTENCES	SPELLING	GROUP PLANNING	ORGANIZING	OUTLINING	SETTING OBJECTIVES	SELECTING TOPICS

© 1997 by The Center for Applied Research in Education, Inc.

SKILLS CHART: RESEARCH

PROBLEM SOLVING					SELF-DISCIPLINE										SELF-EVALUATION				PRESENTATION								
DIVERGENT-CONVERGENT-EVALUATIVE THINKING	FOLLOWING & CHANGING PLANS	IDENTIFYING PROBLEMS	MEETING DEADLINES	WORKING w/LIMITED RESOURCES	ACCEPTING RESPONSIBILITY	CONCENTRATION	CONTROLLING BEHAVIOR	FOLLOWING PROJECT OUTLINES	INDIVIDUALIZED STUDY HABITS	PERSISTENCE	SHARING SPACE	TAKING CARE OF MATERIALS	TIME MANAGEMENT	WORKING WITH OTHERS	PERSONAL MOTIVATION	SELF-AWARENESS	SENSE OF "QUALITY"	SETTING PERSONAL GOALS	CREATIVE EXPRESSION	CREATING STRATEGIES	DIORAMA & MODEL BUILDING	DRAWING & SKETCHING	POSTER MAKING	PUBLIC SPEAKING	SELF-CONFIDENCE	TEACHING OTHERS	WRITING